100 Ideas for Early Years Practitioners:

Supporting Children with SEND

Susan O'Connor

BLOOMSBURY EDUCATION

LONDON OXFORD NEW YORK NEW DELHI SYDNEY

BLOOMSBURY EDUCATION
Bloomsbury Publishing Plc
50 Bedford Square, London, WC1B 3DP, UK
29 Earlsfort Terrace, Dublin 2, Ireland

BLOOMSBURY, BLOOMSBURY EDUCATION and the Diana logo are
trademarks of Bloomsbury Publishing Plc

First published in Great Britain, 2020 by Bloomsbury Publishing Plc

A catalogue record for this book is available from the British Library

ISBN: PB: 978-1-4729-7235-4; ePDF: 978-1-4729-7234-7;
ePub: 978-1-4729-7232-3

2 4 6 8 10 9 7 5 3

Typeset by Newgen KnowledgeWorks Pvt. Ltd., Chennai, India
Printed and bound in the UK by CPI Group (UK) Ltd, Croydon CR0 4YY

To find out more about our authors and books visit
www.bloomsbury.com and sign up for our newsletters

Contents

Acknowledgements

I would like to say thank you to all the people – children and adults – whom I have worked with in nurseries, schools, colleges and other professional institutions and organisations over the last 30 years.

I would also like to thank the publishing team at Bloomsbury, especially Hannah Marston, Chloe Fitzsimmons and Sarah Jacobs for their guidance and support.

Introduction

Special educational needs and disabilities, otherwise known as SEND, encompass both learning difficulties and disabilities. According to the Children and Families Act 2014, a child is considered to present with SEND if they have 'a significantly greater difficulty in learning than the majority of others the same age' or have 'a disability which prevents or hinders them from making use of facilities of a kind generally provided for others of the same age'. More specifically, the 'SEND Code of Practice: 0-25 years' (NASEN, 2015) breaks SEND into four broad areas:

- cognition and learning
- communication and interaction
- physical and sensory
- social, emotional or mental health.

These four areas, and the detail about what they include, are explored further in Idea 2. It is important to remember, however, that every child is unique and will have their own individual needs as they move through your setting.

Difficulties and needs may present at different stages of a child's development. One child's needs might already have been identified when they join the setting, but for other children, it might be that they are spotted later on in the nursery or the Early Years classroom. Some children require SEND support right the way through the Foundation Stage and beyond, while others need targeted support and overlearning for just a short period of time. Sometimes, the teaching of strategies, for example, getting dressed or learning to share, makes a huge difference to a child.

The Equality Act requires all settings to make reasonable adjustments for children with disabilities and the 'SEND Code of Practice: 0-25 years' specifies key guidance around SEND for maintained Early Years settings. This includes, for example, having a qualified teacher in the role of special educational needs coordinator (SENDCo) and ensuring every child is assigned a key person, responsible for meeting their individual needs on a daily basis. It is also essential that settings work closely with parents, carers, outside agencies and other professionals. Remember that parents know their child far better than anyone else. Parents have a key role to play, and effective communication between home and practitioners in the setting is paramount. Nursery (or school) leaders and SENDCos have a responsibility to ensure the setting is compliant with these requirements. However, it is also essential that all practitioners within a setting are practitioners for *all* children, and this means that every member of staff has a responsibility to support children with SEND. It is also important to support parents who are struggling with their child's additional needs.

I wrote this *100 Ideas* book in response to questions from individual practitioners seeking advice and practical ideas for supporting children with SEND in the Foundation Stage. Over my teaching career, I have been a Reception teacher and a SENDCo; I have taught individuals and small groups, and have trained and worked with other professionals in multi-disciplinary teams (including medical professionals, occupational therapists, physiotherapists, speech and language therapists, and educational psychologists). Through these multiple roles, I have developed the tried-and-tested ideas I share in this book, which are easy to implement and ready to use, and do not need any specialist equipment. The ideas will support children with SEND to develop specific skills they may be having difficulties with and help them to progress in your setting. Many of the practical ideas and suggestions are relevant for all Foundation Stage children, but have specific benefits for those with additional needs.

It is important to recognise children's strengths, individual differences and individual variations. One child might be showing early signs of dyslexia with difficulties with language and visual skills; another child might also have early signs of dyslexia and be experiencing difficulties with communication, working memory and processing. Every child is unique and there is no one profile.

It cannot be emphasised enough the benefit babies and children gain from learning through movement, music, art and using their creative skills. They need to be outside, inside, moving, speaking and listening, developing their language skills, listening and enjoying books, learning social skills, taking turns and working with other children to explore their environment. They need to develop the skills of transferring their learning and building on previous tasks and talking about it too – whether it was in the mud kitchen or on the bikes outside! The book is therefore divided into sections around key skills that need to be developed in the Foundation Stage, with each section including fun, varied, multi-sensory activities that bring learning to life for children.

I hope you find the ideas useful, exciting and engaging as you support children with SEND and help them to grow, develop and progress in your setting.

How to use this book

This book includes quick, easy and practical ideas for you to dip in and out of to help you support children with special educational needs and disabilities in your Early Years setting.

Each idea includes:

- a catchy title, easy to refer to and share with your colleagues
- an interesting quote linked to the idea
- a summary of the idea in bold, making it easy to flick through the book and identify an idea you want to use at a glance
- a step-by-step guide to implementing the idea.

Each idea also includes one or more of the following:

Teaching tip

Practical tips and advice for how and how not to run the activity or put the idea into practice.

Taking it further

Ideas and advice for how to extend the idea or develop it further.

Bonus idea ★

There are 26 bonus ideas in this book that are extra-exciting, extra-original and extra-interesting.

Share how you use these ideas and find out what other practitioners have done using **#100ideas**.

Getting it right

Part 1

Supporting children with SEND and their parents and carers

'How can parents see and experience how well children with SEND are welcomed and supported in the setting?'

Effective communication and open working partnerships are vital. There must be an inclusive approach to receiving children with additional needs in line with the SEND Code of Practice 2015 and the Equality Act 2010. The child needs to be at the centre, being supported, with their individual needs being met.

Teaching tip

Locate a SEND Noticeboard in a prominent place for all to see that children and their families are welcome and supported. Often parents and carers will have felt isolated before joining the setting. One idea to include on the noticeboard is to promote coffee mornings and organise information sessions where parents can meet and talk with other parents and other professionals. Share information on how they can best support their child's learning at home.

How do parents and others know about the support that is offered? Is there information on the website or on a SEND noticeboard in the setting? Is it reinforced by leaflets or handouts and by presentations given by the SENDCo or key person?

Do parents know:

- what is meant by SEND and the legal requirements?
- how children with SEND are identified early and their needs are met as part of the 'graduated approach' (assess, plan, do, review)?
- what 'reasonable adjustments' are?
- what support is offered to the child and parents/families/carers?
- who the SENDCo and the child's key person are?
- how the setting works closely with outside agencies and other professionals – local authority advisors, health professionals (e.g. consultant paediatricians, health visitors, speech and language therapists, occupational therapists, physiotherapists), social workers and educational psychologists?

- the 'local offer' website (services, facilities, organisations and activities)?
- what an educational, health and care plan (EHCP) is?
- the contact details of national and local support networks?

The National Network of Parent Carer Forums provides support for parents, carers and families across England and also provides details of local forum groups.

Discuss as a staff team what you can do to further improve engagement and a sense of partnership with parents and carers. Always listen carefully to what parents and carers tell you about home life and routines, relationships and behaviour. Very often you can support parents and carers by suggesting changes to routines or offering new strategies to help young children.

What SEND training is available to staff? Do they attend courses or listen to webinars, or are they members of EYFS SEND cluster groups? Do staff make home visits to discuss needs prior to the child attending the setting? What specialist resources are available to use with the children (for practitioners and parents)?

How inclusive is the setting (policies, routines, planning, attitudes, access – environment, resources, facilities, etc.)? It is vital to hear the views and experience of other users outside the setting and make constant improvements.

Taking it further

Regularly review with parents and all concerned whether the 'planned interventions' and the 'intended outcomes' have effectively supported the child to thrive and progress to the next stage.

SEND training

'How can others (employers, governors and specialists) become aware of the wide range of needs in the setting and the importance of further training in these areas?'

It is vital to keep up to date with current practice and legislation and to meet with employers, practitioners and other professionals in multi-disciplinary fields.

Teaching tip

Clearly identify the areas of training that are needed but also the benefits of the links that can be made and the joint training that can be provided working with multi-disciplinary teams and other professionals.

Arrange regular meetings and invite these people to observe and talk with children, parents and carers, and staff. Explain that some children will just need support for a short period, while other children will need more specialist long-term support or adaptations. Give a brief outline of the areas of SEND and the training that staff have received in these areas. You could refer to the areas defined in the SEND Code of Practice (2015):

- Communication and interaction – children may have a delay or disorder in one or more of the following areas: attention/interaction skills, understanding/receptive language, speech or expressive language.
- Cognition and learning – children may have difficulties with, for example, language, memory and reasoning, sequencing, understanding of number, information processing, problem-solving or fine and gross motor skills.
- Social, mental and emotional – children may have difficulties with, for example, attention, anxiety, behaviour or self-esteem.
- Sensory and/or physical – children may have a medical or genetic condition, for example, visual/hearing impairment, medical condition, physical accessing, sensory processing or self-care.

Being a good communicator

'Some staff are better at talking to the children than others.'

It is important for practitioners to know how to support and develop the children's speech, language and communication skills.

Look at how the children's language skills are tracked, assessed and developed. How are the children's speaking, understanding, listening and attention levels assessed? What are the early interventions? Use the 'graduated approach' actions – assess, plan, do, review – to help identify future communication targets for the children. For example, do the team:

- talk with the children, rather than at them, and give them time to think and respond?
- talk with the children about their interests, hobbies and experiences?
- communicate using a signing/symbol method of communication where needed?
- ask open as well as closed questions and promote good listening skills?
- give a running commentary (a narrative) of children's actions and possible thoughts and ideas?
- introduce new words and provide real-life practical activities that prompt lively debate and conversation?

Discuss the positive 'good communicator' skills already used by the team and decide on actions to be taken to get to know the children even more. Talk more with parents/carers, sharing and discussing assessments with them and outside agencies (if appropriate). How can even more time be allocated to talking with the children and having meaningful conversations? Look for opportunities to have 'interplay conversations', where the child and practitioner conversation builds each time on what was previously said by both.

Teaching tip

Discuss practitioners' communication skills as a team. What opportunities are there for practitioners to learn new strategies to improve their communication skills?

Taking it further

Discuss and decide on actions to provide more weekly information to parents and carers about what the children have been doing. Consider how practitioners have been enabling the children and how they can further develop the children's language and learning, as well as how parents and carers can further support their children's communication skills at home.

Role models

'EYFS asks that we encourage the children to keep going when things get tricky, which we do. What other ways are there?'

Promoting resilience with children of such a young age is important. The skills and attributes they learn in the setting will be foundations that carry them through their future lives.

One idea is to be aware of and foster the culture of creativity in the setting. EYFS has always focused on multi-sensory learning, and this benefits all the children, not just those with SEND. Develop an environment where all practitioners and children can thrive.

Practitioners are very creative (even those who say they aren't!). They will often discuss ideas for future projects, designs for gifts for the children to make and take home, and displays developing themes or that show the children's work. Sometimes practitioners will talk about these topics during the day; ideas will be exchanged and displays created. Children listen to these adult conversations while playing or completing activities. Sometimes the children will stop and be curious or stand and watch part of a display being made.

Develop these great opportunities to reinforce how adults work and are creative. Sometimes the adults might say, 'I'm not sure whether this will work. Perhaps I need to change this. Can you think of any other ways?' The children will see the adults first hand struggling with a task, developing ideas, asking for others' opinions, being innovative, taking risks, trying things out, keeping going, etc.

Planning next steps

'When I'm working with a child, how can I keep in mind assessment for learning and next steps?'

A practitioner's in-depth knowledge of a child's development (strengths and weaknesses) in the prime areas is crucial. So too is knowledge of the child's interests, their likes/dislikes, their relationships, their play and their involvement in learning. What does a child know and understand and what can they do?

These assessments are strengthened by daily communication with parents and carers. Organising regular meetings with all concerned – parents, practitioners and other professionals (speech and language therapists, occupational therapists, physiotherapists, health professionals, educational psychologists, etc.) – is vital in order to discuss a child's overall progress and set targets.

One idea to help with observing and collecting information for use in assessment and planning is to use the acronym 'MORE SPECIAL':

Motivated and manipulating the activities and information
Opportunities – is the child taking up opportunities?
Relationships – developing positive relationships with other children and adults
Exploring and experimenting

Senses – using them to learn
Problem-solving
Embedding experiences
Curious
Interests – what are they?
Adapting to changes
Language – using and extending their language skills

Record observations and data as soon as possible on digital assessment tools.

> **Teaching tip**
>
> Look at how the equipment and physical environment supports the child's learning. Is it meeting the individual needs of the child? If it isn't, adapt or change it so that it does.

> **Bonus idea** ★
>
> Parents and other professionals provide valuable information and advice on possible next steps to take with the child. So too do other practitioners in the setting. Always see it from the child's perspective and ask the child to tell you or show you what they know and understand but perhaps cannot do... yet!

Planning next steps

Fine and gross motor skills, and physical and sensory needs

Part 2

Mark-making and colouring

'A child in nursery avoids anything to do with pencils or crayons. He will push them away. How can we make it more interesting for him?'

Children need to play and develop their fine motor skills before writing begins. Organise a range of activities that develop them. Mark-making, doodling shapes and colouring improves the strength in children's fingers and hands.

Teaching tip

When they are colouring in, encourage the children to improve precision by colouring inside the lines. This develops their hand–eye co-ordination and fine motor skills for later, when they start learning to actually write on a line.

Bonus idea ★

Put out small world play people to encourage working together and discussion.

Preparation is key. Children's hands and muscles need to get used to controlling and producing marks on paper before they start writing letters and words. The children have to be developmentally ready. Mark-making requires physical strength, co-ordination, thought and spatial awareness. Provide a range of surfaces for the children to practise on.

Talk with the children about what they are interested in, e.g. nature, superheroes, space or cars. Draw outlines of superheroes, leaves, flowers, rockets or stars for them to colour in on different surfaces. Draw outlines of racing tracks or roads for the children to add to. Leave toy cars, trucks, tractors or buses for them to drive along the roads. Draw vertical, horizontal or diagonal lines. Add outlines of different shapes – squares, circles, triangles, etc. – for the children to colour in between the lines.

Display different chalks and writing materials for the children to use, e.g. fat chalk sticks, first-grip-style crayons, metallic wax crayons, paint, rollers or sticks. Give children opportunities to draw on tablets or smartboards.

Also remember that taking rubbings of tree bark and a range of other different rough surfaces strengthens hand muscles. Heavy rubbing work increases a child's proprioception.

Threading and squeezing

'Threading, squeezing and using fastenings are difficult for some children.'

Fine motor skills are vital in the development of young children. Threading and squeezing develops the muscles in small hands. Children need to learn how to use zips and undo fastenings, buttons, poppers and Velcro™.

Well-known ideas for threading are:

- threading pieces of pasta onto a lace to create a necklace
- threading beads onto a string
- pushing breakfast cereal (e.g. hoop-shaped pieces) onto spaghetti.

They all require small hands to hold and manipulate the lace, string or spaghetti through the hole.

Another idea is to ask the children to thread coloured spaghetti through the holes of an upturned colander and attach large squidgy eyes to the front to make it into an alien monster! Alternatively, use some coloured salt dough for the children to shape and mould into a hedgehog. Show the children how to break off pieces of spaghetti and insert them into the body to make them into the spikes of the hedgehog.

For practising squeezing, put a variety of fidget balls and rubber toys in an opaque bag. Invite the children to pass the bag around and squeeze one toy or fidget ball in the bag. Watch closely to make sure that there is no peeping! Ask the children to tell everyone what it feels like, the shape or what it might be – for example, a frog. Then encourage the children to take it out of the bag to see whether they were right.

> **Teaching tip**
>
> Give young children and babies opportunities to roll, shake, turn, pull, spin, stack and slide objects and toys, as they can learn to make vital connections about how things work and react.

> **Bonus idea**
>
> Create a 'fastenings box' that contains a variety of shapes and sizes of zips. Select different examples of material and pieces of young children's clothing that have buttons, ties, Velcro™ and poppers to 'do' and 'undo'.

Rhymes and actions

'I like singing rhymes with my friends.'

Reciting and singing rhymes supports children's language learning. Adding actions to the rhymes helps the children to remember them and works on improving their fine motor skills.

Nursery rhymes help to develop an understanding of the rhythms of language. The advantage is that they can be repeated again and again, reinforcing the way words work. One idea is to create new rhymes and actions for existing tunes. The following rhyme can be sung to the tune of 'Incy Wincy Spider' (actions in italics).

Wriggly, wraggly worm
(*Move hands, side to side, in front of body*)

Climbed up the slide
(*Hands 'climb' up imaginary slide*)

Down came the child (whooosh!)
(*Right hand in sharp downwards movement*)

And pushed the worm outside
(*Hands together, then push outwards*)

Out shone the moon
(*Fingers/hands outstretched*)

The children went away
(*Index and middle fingers 'walk away'*)

Wriggly, wraggly worm
(*Move hands, side to side, in front of body*)

Climbed the slide to play
(*Hands 'climb' up imaginary slide*)

Fine motor skills survey

'A small group of children have no interest in pencil or sitting-down activities and will avoid them. One child even asks others to complete colouring tasks for her rather than do them herself.'

Fine motor skills are crucial to performing everyday tasks. They are important for a child's independence and self-esteem.

Create a simple survey on an A4 sheet with tick boxes and room for comments, observations and action points. This can be used as background information for assessment or if the child needs to be referred for specialist help. Can the child perform these tasks?

- Use pencils (Do drawings appear immature?)
- Practical activities (e.g. play outdoor games, play with sand/water)
- Use scissors
- Play with constructional toys (e.g. building blocks, jigsaws)
- Dressing (e.g. tying shoelaces, doing up zips)
- Eating (is the child a messy eater? Can the child open lunch boxes?)
- Hygiene (e.g. cleaning teeth, toileting)
- Use ICT (e.g. use of mouse)

Observe the child's speed and accuracy. Did they have any difficulties? What support could be given to help them? What needs further practice? What help can be given in the setting? This might include further opportunities to practise the skills above or following a commercial fine motor skills programme. It might involve working with a specialist teacher or working on an individual programme with other professionals, for example, occupational therapists.

> **Teaching tip**
>
> Always be open to the possibility of other factors affecting a child's learning, e.g. their fine motor skills might be affected by visual perception difficulties (in seeing and interpreting information).

Isolating finger movements

'This group has difficulties with fine motor skills, particularly using their individual fingers.'

Fine motor skills are very important. Isolating finger movements can help children to develop finger dexterity.

Taking it further

Depending on age and ability, show the children how to 'finger walk'. Ask them to move two fingers in turn across the grid to the first square, press the 'button', then walk to the next square, press and so on.

Fine motor skills are developing when children are, for example, playing games, getting dressed or using a knife and fork. Identify where the children can develop their finger skills further. For example, during art and craft time, children could try:

- sticking down pieces of coloured paper
- using a crayon or a paintbrush
- drawing with a coloured pencil
- pinching material together
- squeezing a tube of glitter
- scrunching together pieces of tissue paper
- gluing and pressing down
- unscrewing and screwing lids on pots.

Sometimes children need to isolate specific fingers. To help with this, play the 'Pressing Squares' game. Draw a large 5 x 5 square grid and draw different pictures in each square. Decide beforehand which fingers or thumbs are going to be focused on. Ask children to come up one at a time to play the game. Check to make sure the children know which is their right and left hand, which are their thumbs and the names of the other fingers. Show and tell the children which hand and finger/thumb you want them to use, e.g. 'With your thumb on your right hand, press all the squares on the board that have a picture of a polar bear.' Resist telling children how many pictures of the polar bear there are to make it more challenging for them and the children who are watching.

Bonus idea ★

To practise isolating fingers, encourage children to press buttons on a keypad, play a musical instrument or press a doorbell.

Snip! Snip!

'Cutting skills are a difficulty.'

Some children use both hands for cutting: they haven't found their dominant hand yet. However, children will become much more successful at cutting when they find that their dominant hand cuts and their non-dominant hand manipulates the paper.

Check that the child is using an appropriate scissor grasp. Well-known advice is that on the dominant hand, the child's thumb should be facing upwards and placed in the top loop of the scissors. The index/middle finger should be placed within the bottom loop. On the non-dominant hand (sometimes called the 'helper hand'), the child's thumb should be facing upwards, with the supporting hand holding the card or paper. If the child struggles to manipulate the card, it could be that either they need more practice at this skill or their bilateral co-ordination is poor.

Check that the child has a good grasp–release motion. If not, practise grasping and releasing with a range of rubber balls.

Demonstrate snipping movements and ask the child to snip off the edges of a card (with their 'helper hand' holding the card). As the child progresses, encourage them to cut further into the card and along 'drawn-in' straight lines. Mark with a pen where you want them to stop. Once straight lines have been mastered, start cutting with a change of direction, turning the paper with the 'helper hand' and then continuing cutting in a new direction.

Practise cutting squares and triangles, then stars. Some children find it easier to progress from straight lines to curves. Practise cutting curves, circles, then spirals.

Teaching tip

Different types of scissors can also help with cutting:

- first scissors
- self-opening scissors
- left-handed scissors
- soft grip scissors.

Cutting shapes and then spirals really tests a child's hand-eye co-ordination and their ability to use the 'helper hand'.

Pencil grip

'There is a Reception child who kneels on his seat to write and has a very awkward pencil grip. His parents feel that the school should be correcting this but he is resistant.'

Sometimes different people in a child's life have views on handwriting and the correct pencil grip to use. Only when a child is developmentally ready should they start learning to write. Some schools encourage the use of the dynamic tripod grip (where the pencil is pinched between the ball of the thumb and the forefinger and is supported by the middle finger, with the other fingers tucked into the hand). However, this does not meet the individual needs of many children, and a different grip is often more effective and comfortable. It is important to find out what works best for the child.

Taking it further

If you have serious concerns, talk with the parents, who might decide that they need to have advice from an occupational therapist or physiotherapist.

Start by observing the child's movements. Ask them to throw a ball into a bucket or hit a ball with a bat. Hand them a play knife and fork and ask them to pretend to eat. Do they swap over the knife and fork or prefer to use just the fork as it is more comfortable? Are they still quite young for the age group? Do they use different hands for different tasks or do they use both? Do they appear to have a dominant hand? Do the practitioners have other concerns about the child or is it just about handwriting? Discuss this with parents/carers.

Check that the table is at an appropriate height and that the chair is correctly sized. The child's feet should be on the floor and their knees bent to about 90 degrees. However, some children are more comfortable with adjustments made to this. Try out commercially available aids:

- triangular pencils or tripod grips
- slightly angled writing boards
- weighted wrist bands
- left- or right-handed pencils and scissors
- perceptual and motor skills programmes.

Letter formation

'Forming letters is a challenge for three children.'

Letter formation can vary from setting to setting, so make sure that children are forming their letters in the same way. A multi-sensory approach helps children to learn.

Start by encouraging good pencil control with precise strokes and movements, identifying the letters that are not yet secure. Ask the children to write out the letters of the alphabet in groups of three or four letters on a small whiteboard. Observe and record any difficulties that the children might have with the formation of these letters.

Talk with the children about whether they have any difficulties with particular letters. Ask them to 'air write' the letters. Use wooden, stone or commercial 'squidgy' letters, where the children can feel and trace the shape of the letter (you can buy 'Feels-Write Letter Stones' from Yellow Door and 'Squidgy Sparkle Gel Letters' from TTS, for example). Sometimes children have difficulty remembering where to start or where to end, or whether it's an anti-clockwise or clockwise movement, a diagonal stroke, or has a zigzag pattern.

Make a letter formation sheet for 'tricky letters'. Create each letter with dotted lines that the children can write over. The individual letters should all have a red dot to start and a green dot to finish. Ask the children to finger trace over the letters and coloured dots, saying 'start' and 'stop'. Ask them to look at the shape and 'feel' in their finger the movement as they are tracing. Check that they are using a finger on the hand that they normally use to write; otherwise they could become confused.

Correct size

'Two children have great difficulty writing correctly sized letters. How can we make learning fun?'

It is difficult for children when they are learning to write. They need to remember how to form letters and write them in the correct size on the base line.

Start by checking that the children know how to form their letters. Ask the children to write out the letters on a small whiteboard as the practitioner says them. Observe and make a record of any difficulties the children might have with the formation of these letters. Ask the children whether they find any letters 'tricky'. Practise 'air writing' and then forming these letters with the children on their whiteboards.

Ask children to write different sizes of a particular letter on a piece of card. Cut the letters out and mix them all up on the carpet. Ask children to work together to put the letters in order from the smallest to the largest. Do they know what 'smallest' and 'largest' means? Point to where you want the children to start and go to! Then mix up the letters and challenge the children to rearrange the letters from the largest to the smallest.

This time, write ten different same-sized letters on cards and cut them out. Draw a long black line on a large piece of card. Place a letter card in the wrong place on the writing line and ask children to tell you if it is right. If they say 'no', ask them to move it to the right place. (Attach it to the large piece of card with sticky tack.) This is a fun game, giving the children confidence. They love 'being the teacher'!

Direction of movement

'A child has started to mirror write. How can we help with direction?'

Occasionally, children 'mirror write' letters and numbers or begin their work from the right-hand side across to the left-hand side of the page. This can indicate that their area of perception or 'position in space' is delayed, but for many children they need to develop their control when moving in clockwise and anti-clockwise directions.

For some letters, children need to move their pencil in an anti-clockwise direction, for example, a, o and c, or in a clockwise direction, for example, b, m and p. Some letters need both clockwise and anti-clockwise movements, for example, s, z and y.

In a hall or large space, ask children whether they know in what direction the hands on a clock move. Check that they understand what 'direction' and 'hands on a clock' mean. Ask them to show you using their hands, as some children have been so used to seeing digital displays that they might not have noticed! Explain and demonstrate to the children (using your arms) that they are going to move in a clockwise way (like a clock) and then in an anti-clockwise way.

Another idea is to demonstrate (with your back turned to the children) a chosen letter by 'walking out' across the hall/floor to feel its movement and direction (formation). It is important that you do not face the children when you are 'walking it out', as this will confuse them, particularly those who have direction difficulties! Ask children to walk out different letters. Observe, help and take note of the children who find this tricky. Record the letters that cause the most difficulties and include these in your future planning.

> **Taking it further**
>
> Reinforce these large movements and directions on a smaller scale. Provide trays of sand or sequins for children to 'finger write' the individual letters in. Give them sticky glue or different paints and paintbrushes to make the movements. Finger-trace different letter shapes. Encourage children to have fun outside using coloured chalks and squirty bottles.

Poor proprioception

'Parents have been told by the occupational therapist that their child is not "processing proprioceptive input" well. He has difficulties with co-ordination and puts a lot of effort into tasks. How can we help him in the setting?'

Proprioception is knowing what the body is doing – the position and load on the muscles and joints (processing sensory information when the body moves). It helps with balance by supporting the vestibular sense to ensure that the child does not fall over.

Teaching tip

Each child is different so see what works for them. Too much activity can sometimes make a child too tired, so match the range of activities to their individual needs. Give rewards to the child for their ongoing persistence and effort!

Talk with the parents and arrange to have a meeting with the occupational therapist and all concerned. Observe the child and ask other practitioners for their observations. What are the signs? Are they leaning on walls or tables? Do they slump down onto their chair? Does the child get tired easily in lessons? Do they spill or drop items? Be aware that their body will respond differently to others. Does the child bump into other children inside and outside the room? Do they find it difficult to gauge the correct force or speed when playing with toys or running?

What strategies in the setting can be put in place to help the child learn and thrive? Well-known activities to stimulate the proprioceptive sense include taking or grasping, squeezing, pushing, pulling, lifting, climbing and stretching, so encourage the child to:

- roll out and squeeze playdough
- use construction bricks to snap, push and pull apart
- kick, push and hit balls into hoops or buckets
- catch and throw beanbags and balls
- use the gardening equipment to push, dig, water and plant
- use outside large play equipment to climb and stretch
- swim, run or jump.

Balance and co-ordination

'The physiotherapist has recommended that two children need to build up their balance and co-ordination when playing in the outside area. We have ride-on toys, spinning cones and roundabouts. What else can we encourage them to use?'

Balancing helps children to develop sensory integration and muscle response. One idea is to use balance steps, a floor surfer, see-saws or balance/wobble boards to improve their balance.

Balance steps are often multicoloured and can be positioned on the ground to create stepping stones for the children to balance and walk on. Ask the children to lay the 'steps' on the ground and see whether they can create a bendy path!

Floor surfers are on wheels. The child lies on their tummy and co-ordinates their legs and arms to push on the ground and move themselves around (depending on the age of the child). Ask the other children to experiment with using small cones to make a 'track' that the child can move along without bumping into the cones. Check that it is wide enough to get through!

Climbing on, moving in the air and getting off a see-saw require good balancing skills. Ask the children to count how many times they touch the ground and then challenge them to see whether they can beat their score the next time.

Wobble boards can be used to improve balance and co-ordination when sitting, kneeling or standing on them. Give the children a clipboard and pencil and ask them to use a child's stopwatch (or a timer on a tablet) to time how long they can balance on the board. Ask them to experiment with rocking forwards, backwards and from side to side.

> **Teaching tip**
>
> To make it more of a challenge when the children are on the wobble board, ask them to copy a practitioner's hand movements or sing and rehearse action songs!

Navigating around the world!

'There are children who are always tripping over or bumping into desks or objects. They continually have difficulty packing their bags to go to PE or to go home in the afternoon.'

Spatial skills help us to navigate around the world and to understand the relationships between objects, making sense of dimensions. Motor skills, sound processing and visual processing all contribute to children's proprioception.

Taking it further

An idea to test whether children know their 'spatial language' is to make use of hand actions. Play the balloon game. Give each child a balloon and ask them to 'put the balloon *in front of* your body', then '*behind* your body', etc. This is a great observation exercise. Ask one of the children to 'be the teacher' and observe which spatial instructions different children find tricky and then reinforce that with them.

Create activities where children need to navigate from A to B, with obstacles to walk around (e.g. chairs or cones). Point from where you are now to where you are going to. Tell the children to imagine starting at A and following the route to B, going around the chairs or cones. Choose different children to navigate their way around the chairs or cones.

1 Ask the children whether they can rearrange the chairs and make a different route from A to B. Tell them that it is like using a video in your head. Explain to them that good thinking means that you often think about and then plan a route, using your imagination and your 'mind's eye'.

2 Using their own small whiteboard and pen, ask children to write A at the bottom of their whiteboard and B at the top. Draw in the chairs and draw the line around them from A to B. Now, using their plan, can they lay out the chairs or cones in the room and move around them in the correct order on their map without bumping into them?

3 In pairs, can children create simple maps for other children to follow, using a start point, an end point and various obstacles (chairs) along the way?

This is an ideal opportunity to use and integrate spatial language into the day by giving instructions, e.g. 'in front of', 'beside', 'next to', 'behind', 'between', 'to the left', 'on the right', 'above' and 'underneath'.

Alternatively, play a 'find the toy' game. Place toys around the setting before the children arrive. Create cards with directions that the children have to follow to find the toys (the practitioner reads the cards aloud). Use spatial language, for example, 'Walk between the two red chairs and look inside the box.'

Bonus idea

Allow extra time when changing for PE and show the children how to fold their clothes neatly. Using their spatial skills, can they pack their shoes and clothes into a suitcase/bag? Can they pack them into a rucksack? Another idea is to bring a packed lunchbox into the setting and open and empty the contents out onto a table. Can children pack all the items neatly into the lunchbox without squashing them and then close the lid?

Misses the ball

'It's really difficult for some children to enjoy playing games with others and feel good about themselves when they can't catch or hit a ball with a bat and they're constantly dropping things.'

Hand—eye co-ordination develops over time (going well into the primary school years). Some young children are able to put their hands out in front of them and 'body catch' a ball. For others, this takes a lot longer.

Before the children arrive, set up two or more of the following activities, so that children can move around them in small groups.

- Rolling: Use a range of different weights and different-sized coloured balls to roll into large upturned buckets.
- Throwing: Use brightly coloured beanbags to throw into buckets or hoops.
- Catching (or running after and picking up!): Use brightly coloured, large balls to start with.
- Bat and ball: Use a 'children's style' cricket bat or hockey stick to guide balls around a line of coloured skittles (or beanbags) and hit into buckets at the end.

Tell the children that they are going to play 'activity circle' and demonstrate the different activities to them. What do they need to focus on? Show them how to plan their movements. What hand/wrist/arm movements do they need to make? Do they need to swivel their hands, twist, turn or rotate their fingers? Do they need to grasp, throw or push?

Be patient, as learning new skills does take more time than you think. All the skills of hand—eye co-ordination (working together) — manipulation, rhythm and precision — are important in learning.

Balance bikes and tricycles

'A child in the setting needs to improve her gross motor skills and will not use the outdoor bikes. She lacks confidence and will not try. How can we encourage her?'

Riding on bikes and tricycles helps to improve gross motor skills — the large muscle groups of the body that enable walking, running, balance and co-ordination.

Balance bikes or ride-on bikes are bikes with no pedals. Encourage the child to just sit on one and gain confidence. Later on, they can learn to steer and concentrate on moving at the pace they want to, without having to pedal.

The child could progress to a tricycle (where they need to both steer and peddle). At this stage, if the child is nervous, just encourage them to balance and move with alternate feet pushing on the ground. Progress with the child's feet on the pedals and the adult pushing from behind (so that the child feels the sensation and movement needed).

Play simple 'stop, go' games with the child to help with speed control. Create a small road track with cones. Introduce traffic lights and crossings to encourage stopping and starting, with obstacles to peddle and steer around. Create a learning environment that the child is interested in. Ask them whether they would like to be a bus driver and drive their passengers to the train station, the swimming pool, the park or the shops. Alternatively, would they like to be a delivery driver and deliver 'goods/parcels' to a school, the shops or a factory? (Many 'bikes' have a compartment on the back where small world people or items/packages could be placed). Introduce bus stops for passengers or parking areas for delivery vans.

> **Teaching tip**
>
> Introduce new skills step by step and at the child's pace. Sometimes the child gets so engrossed in their play and imaginary games that they forget about their previous difficulties and anxieties.

Active breaktimes

'I don't really like breaktime or going outside and running around. I like sitting down inside on my own.'

Some children dislike breaktime and any form of free play. They will linger by the door and be reluctant to go outside in the fresh air, even when encouraged to do so by their playground buddy. It is important to find ways in which they can enjoy themselves, make friends and have fun with movement all at the same time.

First of all, talk with the child. Find out why they don't like breaktime or free play. It can be that they simply don't like games due to their competitive nature, because the games are noisy or because they haven't yet developed friendship groups.

Reassure them that there are times when everybody feels a little bit lonely. If the setting has one, a well-known idea is that they can always go to the 'friendship bench' and find somebody to play with. Some settings might also have playground helpers who wear colourful baseball hats or badges, and who will play a variety of games with the children.

Instead of running from game to game, some children really enjoy getting absorbed in an activity at breaktime. Another idea, as well as providing small equipment – hoops, balls and bats, for example – is to create an area for large constructive play, where the child needs to concentrate and work using their imagination to problem-solve. Building things, taking them apart and then putting them back together again enables them to move around, make friendships and work together with others. Breaktime has a purpose and is more meaningful and enjoyable. It is looked forward to rather than dreaded!

All children love to pretend to be the teacher in their free play. Teach them a range of action songs, where they take turns standing in front of the class. Be dramatic and over-emphasise the actions. Use the same short, catchy instructions: 'And turn to the side... STRETCH!' You will smile or cringe when you hear your words and actions repeated at breaktime!

One well-known action song is 'Head, shoulders, knees and toes', but you could try extending this to:

Feet, ankles, legs and hips,
Legs and hips
Feet, ankles, legs and hips,
Legs and hips
And stomach, elbows, chest and hands,
Feet, ankles, legs and hips
Legs and hips!

Note the following actions for the body parts that are difficult to point to:

For elbows: Cross their hands over their body to touch the opposite elbow with the opposite hand.

For hands: Place hands in front of their body and wave from side to side.

Bonus idea ★

To identify some of the different activities at breaktime, video some of the suggested playground activities and show the children how they are moving and working together. Shy or quiet children are often surprised by their activity.

Using both sides

'I have been asked to work on the children's bilateral integration.'

Bilateral integration is using the right and left side of the body together at the same time or with alternating movements. It plays a vital role in a child's physical development.

Tell children that they are going to play a game called 'Actions gym'. This can be played in groups of two or three while the other children in the setting are busy on their activities. Decide from the list below which well-known activities you are going to observe and assess in the session. Set up the activities in advance.

Alternating movements (first one hand or leg and then the other performs the same movement in a rhythmical way):

- walking up and down stairs
- pedalling a tricycle or similar toy
- skipping.

Symmetrical movements (each hand or leg doing the same action at the same time):

- clapping hands together
- pulling apart construction bricks
- pushing a wheelbarrow.

Leading hand and supporting hand movements (one hand supports the other hand to do the work):

- cutting with scissors (holding the card)
- feeding, using a knife and fork
- threading/lacing beads.

Depending on the group, time the children for an appropriate amount of time, e.g. 30 seconds. Alternatively, the children can time themselves using a simple children's stopwatch or a large sand timer.

Crossing the midline

'As she writes with her right hand, a child will move over the whole of her body to the left-hand side of the paper, to avoid crossing over her body.'

Some children will use the left hand for tasks on the left-hand side of the body and the right hand for tasks on the right-hand side of the body. It is important to cross over the midline of the body with the arms and legs. Both hemispheres of the brain then work together and communicate, to co-ordinate learning and movement.

Well-known activities for crossing the midline include marching games and bat and ball games. Model gently marching on the spot. Demonstrate to children (in stages) how to cross the left hand over the body, raise the right leg and touch the right knee with the left hand. Demonstrate with the other side of the body. Ask children to count and complete the action five times.

Lay out an obstacle course. With a large toy bat and ball, encourage children to weave in and out, gently tapping the ball with the bat from the left-hand side to the right-hand side of the cones.

Another idea to practise crossing the midline is to place card outlines of footprints in front of the whiteboard. Ask the child to stand on the footprints and not move off them. Draw a column of ten red dots on the left side of the board and ten corresponding dots on the right. Ask the child to draw horizontal lines across from one red dot to the other red dot. Make sure they don't swap hands in the middle! The child can choose to start from the right- or left-hand side but the challenge is that they mustn't move their feet off the footprints.

Taking it further

The child could stand on the footprints to play the dressing game, where their clothes are placed on different sides of the footprints. The child bends and stretches over the midline with both hands to reach their clothes. This is a suggestion that could be passed on to parents too.

Working on self-regulation

'A child in my setting displays very high levels of motor activity, with his feet swinging and tapping when seated. He cannot stay in one place. He will often jump from inappropriate heights.'

Children will need supervision and encouragement to stay on task, particularly if they act spontaneously without any sense of danger.

Teaching tip

Create opportunities to work on self-regulation. Sometimes it helps when a child acts spontaneously to teach them to ask themselves the question 'What is everyone doing now?'

Concentrate on lowering frustration levels and increasing self-esteem. Praise children for their efforts. Introduce a reward star chart (on a piece of card) that can be handed to the practitioner at the end of the session and reviewed at the end of the day. Stars can be awarded for listening, concentration and waiting for instructions.

Make the learning environment more comfortable. Check that the seating allows the children to rest both their feet flat on the ground and encourage them to sit upright. The table should be at elbow height. A sloping surface can be used for reading and other activities.

Taking it further

Instead of leaping and running to line up, tell children to listen to the rest of the practitioner's instructions and *then* line up. It just creates a pause, enough to think again about performing an inappropriate action.

Position the children so that they are able to view the practitioner directly without turning their bodies and be close enough to hear and see instructions. They should be sitting where there are minimal distractions, e.g. away from windows or doors or other walkways. When sitting on the floor, if possible, it is a good idea to place the children on the outside edge of the group so that they are able to stretch but are still close enough to see and hear the practitioner's instructions.

Rhythm – clapping, shaking, stamping

'Co-ordination, concentration and body awareness is a problem for some children who are experiencing a range of learning difficulties in the setting. They find it hard to clap a rhythm.'

Children's listening, language and rhythm skills develop by playing games involving sounds. Music, and moving to music, is at the very heart of learning for young children. They need to process the sounds, following the direction and pitch, and keeping a rhythm.

A well-known idea is to clap out the words of poems, rhymes, raps or songs together. It can be made more challenging by adding marching on the spot, stamping, moving forwards and backwards, using whole-body actions and adding pauses (where the children need to count – for example, 1... 2... 3... go).

Another idea is to practise varying the speed or volume. Make it slow, make it fast, make it loud or soft. Instead of the practitioner and everybody doing the clapping together, ask the children to watch and listen to the practitioner giving a clapping rhythm, then ask the children to repeat it back.

Clap above your head, clap below your knees. Clap across your body, to the left, to the right (performing cross-lateral movements). Experiment with humming or singing a tune.

Ask the children to sit in a circle. Go around the circle, asking the first child to clap out a simple rhythm (for example, no more than five claps) and then ask the second child to repeat it.

Develop themes. Use music and songs from different topics, e.g. under the sea, animals, pirates, castles, and dragons and fairy tales.

Bonus idea ★
Make sound shakers using different-sized containers. Fill them with pasta, rice or pebbles. Use bells, tambourines or saucepans and wooden spoons. Bang or shake them. Make it fun!

Physical needs and sensory experience

'What activities can we do on the outdoor equipment to support children with physical needs? How can we make it a more sensory experience?'

Some settings have outdoor climbing frames, slides and walkways that are EYFS-friendly, where the children can climb, hang, swing and slide, but these are not always accessible to all.

One idea is to create a lower-level sensory activity pathway to improve strength, balance and co-ordination, where the children can walk or run – sometimes barefoot – on different surfaces and mediums, such as sand, grass, carpet or child-friendly wood/cork.

The children can be encouraged to experiment. For example:

- climb across a ladder on the ground
- jump onto stepping stones or carpet tiles
- scramble onto large blocks or logs
- step into hoops
- balance by walking along low-level planks
- lift and push a toy wheelbarrow
- jump into tyres
- crawl through tunnels
- jump on tumbling mats
- throw large balls into buckets or dustbins.

Ask the children for their ideas. What other activities could be included in the sensory pathway?

Divide the children into small groups and give them a clipboard, marker pen and a timer. The timer could be a child's toy stopwatch or the timer on a tablet. If appropriate, ask the children to record each child's time in their group and decide who had the fastest time.

Tactile defensiveness

'A child in the nursery has tactile defensiveness and the occupational therapist has recommended that we provide a variety of tactile experiences and record what the child reacts to. His parents are doing the same at home.'

Tactile defensiveness (also known as touch sensitivity) occurs when most everyday touch sensations feel unpleasant or dangerous to the child who is experiencing them. The child may respond suddenly by making noises, running away to a quiet corner of the room, lashing out or refusing to join in.

Firstly, meet with the parents and the occupational therapist. Outline your observations and the strategies you have used so far and ask the therapist for their recommendations. Agree two or three future targets with all concerned, and circulate these to the other practitioners.

When approaching a child from behind, try telling them that you are approaching, rather than surprising them unexpectedly and the child responding inappropriately. Instead of close contact with other children, place the child at the beginning or end of a walking line and/or sitting at the edge of the group at storytime. Prepare the child for movement beforehand by telling them that the group are moving to another area of the setting, going to another room or walking to the park, etc.

Tell the child beforehand what you want them to do – for example, in order to wash their hands, point to the soap, or give the child their own hairbrush to brush their hair. If the child dislikes play activities using tactile materials – water, sand, threading, construction, etc. – arrange for them to be with just one other child or on their own.

Teaching tip

By using these strategies to start with, the aim is to ease the child into developing normal reactions to different tactile sensations. However, for some children it might be that the reactions persist throughout their life.

Sensory play area

'We would like to develop a sensory play/quiet area at our nursery for babies and children with SEND. We know that it would be beneficial to them.'

A sensory play/quiet area benefits all children in the setting, but particularly babies and children with SEND. It is a quiet, calm place away from the noise that children with ASD in particular find so upsetting at times.

First of all, don't rush into buying expensive equipment that isn't required. Find out what your needs are – talk to occupational therapists, other professionals and parents, visit other settings and find out what worked for them in order to produce the best possible outcomes for the children, parents, practitioners and all concerned. Every child and every setting has varying needs and a different layout, so decide what will work for yours.

According to individual needs, review whether it will be used all day or by certain groups at certain times. Will it benefit one-to-ones, small groups of children with practitioners or visiting professionals, or parents in the setting?

Sometimes, settings decide to make the area into a dark den or use different canopies to create a theme.

Ideas for equipment might include bubble and liquid tubes, bricks, fountains, stars, (with fibre-optic mood lights and dimmers), light- and shadow-makers, illuminated writing boards, calming music, reflecting mirrors and chimes, an aromatherapy set, tactile picture books, calming weighted blankets, eco-torches, metallic pebbles, tactile fidget busters, textured cubes and squeezy sensory balls, vibrating calming cushions, sight and sound drums, glow rattles or feely tubs.

Teaching tip

If needed, expensive equipment for the sensory/quiet area can often be acquired through donations or fundraising, but equally, items can be made or acquired at a fraction of the cost. Make items to stack, shake, roll, sort or move (depending on suitability and age of the child) – for example, cushions, mats, rattles, drums or tubs from natural or reclaimed resources.

Sequencing and working memory

Part 3

Sequences

'A number of children have difficulty with sequencing. What activity can I do that is fun and practical and that they will enjoy?'

Sequencing skills are essential for learning, as they make the world more understandable and predictable.

Teaching tip

For some children it helps to lay out the equipment in order of use on the table from left to right. They can then visually sequence each stage of the recipe.

Cooking is one of the best ways to use all the senses for multi-sensory learning – taste, touch, sight, sound and smell. The bright colours of the ingredients and the use of the equipment help the children to remember the different 'steps' of the recipes. Working together and listening to other children's comments often reinforces their sequencing skills. In order to make the recipe, you need to follow the steps in a certain order.

Explain to the children what they are going to 'make' today. Recipes for the following work well:

- veggie wholemeal pizza
- fruit salad
- banana buns.

Ask children whether they know the names of the equipment they are going to use. How do you use them? Have they used them before? Why are they wearing aprons and washing their hands before they start cooking?

As they are cooking or baking, take photographs showing the different steps – ideally six to eight photos, but it can be more. Of course, make sure you take a photo of the final product and the children tasting it! Afterwards, print and laminate the photos onto cards. Ask the children to tell you what is happening in each of the photos.

Ask the children to place the photos in order/ sequence. This is a great opportunity to use positional language – first, second, third, fourth, fifth, sixth and so on. Alternatively, you can use 'to start with', 'then', 'next', 'after that' and 'at the end' or even 'lastly, we...'.

Go through the sequence and write down what the children said on strips of paper. Make a 'scrapbook cookbook'. Ask the children to design the cover, with pictures of some of the ingredients and the cooking equipment they used.

If there is time, talk about the language that is often used in the recipes, e.g. 'weigh', 'add', 'stir in', 'make', 'mix together', 'wash', 'spoon', 'put' and 'lay'.

On the inside cover or the 'author page', ask the children to write/sign their name. The children are very proud to write their name and it reinforces the importance of independent writing. At the end of the scrapbook cookbook, ask children for their comments/reviews. Give examples – 'delicious', 'tasty', 'yummy' or 'I would make this again with more apples!'

The children can take it in turns to take the scrapbook cookbook home to show family members and to tell them how they made the recipe step by step.

Taking it further

Every time you cook a different recipe, take photographs and make the photos into a simple recipe card (Step 1, Step 2, Step 3, etc.) that can be laminated and used for future groups. The children will love to see that their activities have a purpose. It is even more thrilling and meaningful when they know that their little brother or sister will use it a year or so later!

What are we going to be doing next?

'Difficulties remembering the routine of the day is common among the children, even though we have talked to them first thing in the morning. They are constantly asking, "What are we going to be doing next?" or "Is it lunchtime now?"'

By using their senses, this idea helps the children to remember and focus on the day's activities. Particularly on a morning, when arriving at the setting, it can be difficult for children to use their sequencing skills and listen to and remember what activities they are going to do. They might be thinking about a range of things — what happened before coming in to the setting, what they did yesterday, who they want to sit next to or who they want to play with, just for a start!

Teaching tip

Choose a catchy piece of music to 'start' some activities — for example, at the beginning of tidy-up time, the children would hear the music and know that it was time to pack away. This has the benefit of reinforcing their daily routine-sequencing skills without the adult having to say a word!

If the setting has a very busy day planned, with additional activities, it might be appropriate to just tell the children about the morning's activities, rather than outlining the whole day's events. Sometimes, it is just too much information for a young child to recall.

Create simple 'routine of the day' visual picture cards — for example, welcome, maths, music, books, messy play, breaktime, art and craft, making, toilet, wash hands, snack, forest school, cooking, dress up, games, storytime, mark-making/writing, quiet time, gardening, tidy-up time and home time. Laminate the cards and keep them in a special box, which can be opened each day. This builds excitement and expectation. These 'routine of the day' visual picture cards (ideally no more than eight to ten per day) can then be displayed horizontally or vertically on a wall or board from either left to right or top to bottom.

Ask the children to use tactile, hands-on learning by touching and saying what the activity is, from the first card to the last, using their senses to remember and reinforce the sequence of the cards.

Another idea when going through and discussing the order of the cards is to choose different children to act out or mime what you are going to do. For example, for cooking, mime stirring with a wooden spoon. Then ask all the children to join in and stir. This reinforces the activity, as it uses their working memory.

Ask the children whether they are missing any cards. Could they create any more? Do they have any suggestions? Do they have any ideas for the drawings for the other activities they do? Children often have great and highly original ideas that the adults just haven't thought of before.

Taking it further

Some children benefit from having their own selection of laminated 'routine of the day' cards on a keyring. These can be given to parents or carers at home time so that they can prepare the child that evening for the next day's activities. Parents can keep a record of the activities that night and then ask the child the next evening, 'And what did you do today in forest school?' This promotes communication and further reinforcement of working memory and sequencing skills.

Getting dressed

'I don't like getting dressed. It takes a long time.'

Some children have difficulties getting changed for activities. They will put clothing on in the wrong order, and occasionally the left shoe will be on the right foot and the right shoe on the left foot. Often, with practice, they will improve but for some children, getting dressed will always be a struggle. There are simple strategies that help.

One idea is to have pictures that show the order or sequence of tasks that need to be done. The pictures can be laminated on separate cards on a child's keyring or the pictures can be attached to a long piece of card.

Show the child how to look at and follow the order of the pictures. Here's an example for getting changed:

1 Picture of jumper (reminder to take off their jumper, fold it neatly on the desk or hang it on the peg, and put on new clothes)
2 Picture of T-shirt (reminder to take off and fold T-shirt and put on new clothes)
3 Picture of trousers or dress/skirt (personalise this card) (reminder to take off trousers, dress or skirt and put on new clothes)
4 Picture of shoes/trainers (reminder to take off and put on new shoes/trainers)
5 Picture of footprints (reminder to place shoes/trainers under their chair or peg)

Butterflies, frogs and bees!

'Are there simple visual ways to help children who are struggling to understand the concept of order?'

Look to nature. Life cycles of creatures are often described to children.

For young children and those who are finding it difficult to understand the concept of order, make the explanation as visual and real-life as possible. If it's the right time of year and the setting is near a pond, make several visits to it. See the frogspawn and then visit again to see how the froglets and frogs have developed.

Look out for butterflies and bees. Show pictures or video clips and talk to the children about the life cycle of a butterfly:

1 egg on a leaf
2 caterpillar
3 chrysalis (pupa)
4 butterfly.

Create a large four-stage 3D visual display of the butterfly's life cycle (at child level) that the children can touch. Make large props for the display, e.g. use balloons to make papier maché and paint them when dry to represent the eggs. Add large, curved arrows to the display to emphasise the four stages of the butterfly's life cycle and add key words. Ask for volunteers from the children to touch the display and tell the other children about the life cycle. Emphasise that it all happens in order, one stage after the other. Tell the children that you can't jump and miss out a stage as, again, it all happens in order.

Other suggestions for topics where a 3D display of a sequence might be used are frogs (spawn, tadpole, froglet, frog) or oak trees (acorn, seedling, sapling, tree).

Taking it further

This is a working display. Don't worry if it gets a little worn around the edges. As it is at the children's height, it's also great for them to touch the display and tell visitors to the setting about the cycle!

Bonus idea

Commercial 'butterfly gardens' can be purchased, where the children can watch real butterflies develop in a net casing in the room and later the children can release the 'grown butterflies' into nature.

Remembering names

'Remembering and saying names is a difficulty for some children.'

Remembering personal details about themselves and about their peers helps children to improve their identity, sense of belonging and self-esteem.

Start by giving the children a small piece of paper and asking them to draw themselves. (It is the act of 'drawing' themselves that's important, not the end product!) For the children who say they can't do this, just draw a face and ask them to draw in the hair, eyes, nose and mouth. Ask the children to sit in a circle and, one by one, show their picture to the other children and say their name. Start with their first names and then go on to their family name (if appropriate).

Play the name game. Ask children to stand up if their name is 'Muhammad', 'Amina', 'Noah', etc. Make sure that by the end of the game you have asked everyone to stand up. If some children found this difficult, you can play the game again but this time ask them to do an action as well, for example, wiggle like a worm or jump like a frog. The children enjoy the humour!

Do they know the names of other children in the setting? Ask them to stand up and clap their hands if they are sitting next to 'Sarah', 'Russell', 'Rashid', etc. Check first that they understand what 'sitting next to' means. Demonstrate if necessary. Observe the children who just think that it means on their left but not on their right, etc. If there are multiple children with the same name, ask the children how many 'Sarahs' there were, etc. It is interesting to see who was watching and can recall.

Bonus idea ★

Photos help children to remember too. Do the children know the names of the setting's staff? Show the children and ask them, 'Do you know whose photo this is?' Alternatively, place some photos on the floor or a table.

Working memory

'A number of children find it difficult to remember what they have been asked to do and keep repeating errors. They often leave tasks incomplete.'

Poor working memory skills have an impact on children's learning and wellbeing. Children can be supported and shown ways to help them remember and understand.

Often, children cannot remember information or instructions because the person who was talking to them spoke in sentences that were too long. Sometimes the information is meaningless. Keep instructions short. For some children with working memory difficulties, one instruction is enough for them to process and act upon. Always repeat important information and check understanding by asking the children questions about it. Encourage familiarity and tell children to use the memory aids around the setting on displays, posters and laminated word lists.

Explain to the children what important or 'key words' are and why they need to listen for them in a sentence. Ask children to tell you the key words in a chosen sentence – for example, 'Pick up your flower pot and put it outside on the table.' Play a short game with other sentences to practise this skill.

Talk about how colour, shapes, drawings and pictures help children to remember. Play the 'Picture game'. On a sheet of A4 card, draw three large circles. Ask children to think about their favourite toys and why they like playing with them. From shopping catalogues containing large, colourful pictures of toys, ask children to cut out three of their favourite toys. Then ask them to stick one of the pictures in each of the circles on the card. Set a timer (for example, one minute) and ask a child to touch the pictures and tell the rest of the group about them.

Teaching tip

Ask another child to tell the group about the previous child's three toys. Emphasise how listening, talking, playing games, breaking up information and using colours and pictures all help children to remember.

43

A little reminder

'I find just a little reminder helps.'

Children often just need a quick reminder or a prompt. This is an easy way to help them remember and also develop their thinking and language skills.

Teaching tip

Keep reminding the children about these six words that can help them to remember. Ask the children at different times to repeat them.

Tell the children about a child called Jackson who was telling a story about a visit to the seaside. Jackson knew that he had a lot to say but he couldn't remember it all! Ask the children whether they can think of any ideas to help him remember. (The children often have some great ones!)

Tell the children to close their eyes and imagine the letter 'W'. Ask them to draw it in the air with their hand. Ask them to start counting and add four more 'Ws'. How many are there altogether? Check that the children understand what 'altogether' means. Tell the children to imagine an 'H' and draw that letter in the air with their hand. Write five 'Ws' and one 'H' on a large piece of paper. Highlight them or write them in a different colour. Write in the rest of the letters so that it reads:

- Where?
- When?
- What?
- Why?
- Which?
- How?

Talk to the children about the meanings of these words.

Starting with 'Where?', create Jackson's story with the children, asking them 'Where did he go?', 'When did he play on the beach?', 'What happened?', 'Why did he buy a new bucket and spade?', 'Which one did he choose?' and 'How did he make the sandcastle?'

Repeat what you heard

'I think that children remembering what they have just heard needs to be practised more.'

Auditory memory skills are a vital part of a child's learning and development. They are often overlooked in a busy setting.

Auditory memory skills can be practised by playing games that involve following simple instructions. Compile a list of small tasks and actions, such as 'clap your hands twice', that can be completed by the children in the setting. Tell the children that you are going to play the game 'Listen, remember, do'.

It is a good idea to start with short general instructions, such as 'Stand up', 'Clap your hands' or 'Walk to the window'. After children have completed the action or task, can they repeat the instructions to you? Once they have all had a turn, make the instructions more specific, e.g. 'Go over to the red table and sit on a chair.'

Gradually increase the difficulty level and the number of instructions. For example:

- Two instructions: Walk over to the person furthest away from you and shake their hand.
- Three instructions: Walk all the way around the room, clapping your hands, and then say 'hello' to an adult.

The children love to laugh and join in with these games, enjoying being funny and a little silly!

Teaching tip

It is much easier to have the tasks and actions identified first, rather than trying to think of them on the spot. That way, you can observe individual children and assess their auditory memory skills, rather than having to think about what you are going to ask them to do in the next task.

Taking it further

Another idea to extend this game is by handing out a token each time the child follows the instruction correctly. The winner is the child with the most tokens. If the children are really good at this game, you might want to stop at four or five instructions and have several winners, to keep up the pace of the game!

Self-esteem and wellbeing

Part 4

Self-esteem – celebrating individual children

'Some children are fortunate and celebrate their birthdays at home more than others. How can we make birthdays special for all children in the setting?'

All children and adults have a birthday (sometimes the date can be shared with another child, but usually they will have been born at a different time). It is important for the children to know that we are going to celebrate each child's birthday as it is their special day.

Taking it further

On the day of the birthday, happy birthday songs can be sung and children can wear a special badge. Another idea is to make a large card and for all the children to 'sign' their names inside. A special cake could be made during the day. All of these activities help to promote identity and meaningfulness.

Ask children to tell you (in order) the days of the week and the months of the year. One idea is for the children to sit in a circle. One child stands in the middle of the circle and places their hands together away from their body and then 'points' them at one child, then the next, going round the circle, etc. If a child doesn't know the next day/month, then the centre child points at the next child along. For fun, some children like to pretend to be a robot!

Ask the children to tell you when their birthday is. (Before asking, have a prepared list of birthdays to help them if they get stuck. If their birthday is soon, some children tell you in the number of sleeps left!) Do they know the date and month? Explain that birthdays are on a different *day* each year. This is a great way for practitioners to make days and months of the year meaningful.

Create a noticeboard with the months of the year and the children's names and birthdays under the correct month. A photo of the child can be added. Children love to see the practitioner's birthday added under the months too!

Deciding not to speak

'We don't know how to help a child who has recently joined the setting and has decided not to speak. The parents are working with a speech and language therapist, who has said that it is caused by anxiety. Even though they are not talking, the child is making age-appropriate progress.'

Selecting not to talk sometimes happens when a child needs to speak more outside the home. It can be an anxiety disorder and is sometimes called a 'talking phobia' or 'selective mutism'.

It is important to meet with the parents and the speech and language therapist to hear their opinions. Discuss your observations and assessments, then review progress and agree joint targets.

Putting pressure on the child to speak immediately will probably make them worse, so focus on reducing their anxiety and building up their confidence. Don't pressurise them to make eye contact. Speaking in front of a large group in the morning or saying their name at register time will probably be difficult. Create cards or self-registration pictures that they can show or post in a box. Other difficult times might be when greeting, saying please and thank you, answering questions, making choices, talking about their learning, phonics, expressing needs and ideas, reading aloud, or speaking in assemblies or plays. Decide on other non-verbal ways to communicate with adults, e.g. using hand signals. Small rooms or break-out areas make it easier for the child to communicate.

The child might not have difficulties making friends. Sometimes they might whisper and ask their friends to speak for them. Build on this by arranging for the child to work in pairs or friendship groups, as they might then start to talk.

Teaching tip

Encourage whole-group activity by singing songs with actions as well as words. Sometimes a child will overcome their anxiety and suddenly join in a class discussion. In the beginning, try not to draw too much attention to this and just carry on as normal. Acknowledgement of their verbal participation can have the opposite effect and put them off speaking for a while. Reinforce their good ideas later on.

Emotions

'Learning to understand emotions and how to manage feelings is an important part of development. Children find it difficult if another child is crying or shouting.'

It is important for children to learn to deal with their own emotions and those of others. Young children's behaviour often improves when they have found a way to communicate.

Taking it further

If there have been difficulties in the setting between children, this is always a great opportunity to talk to them about why it is important and how it feels inside to say that you are really sorry for what you said or did.

One idea is to talk to the children about when they have felt happy, sad, angry, worried, scared, frustrated, shy or excited. Choose three or four emotions from the list. Check that the children understand what the words mean. Ask them whether they can tell you about what happened and how they felt. Tell them that it is normal and that everybody has feelings and emotions.

Talk with the children about what they could do if they felt like this. It is important for the children to listen to each other and understand the different ways in which they can feel and react in the future. Talk about other feelings and emotions that the children experience in their everyday lives.

Cut out pictures from magazines that clearly show children's feelings and emotions. Laminate the pictures on cards. Ask the children to choose a card and tell the class about how the child in the picture is feeling. Ask the children about how they know.

The kindness tree

'We want to encourage the children to help others.'

It is important for the children to think not just about themselves but also about other children in the setting.

Many children don't yet realise that what they do and what they say have an effect on the wellbeing of themselves and others. Talk to the children about helping and being kind and thoughtful. Ask them whether they know what these words mean.

Ask for two or three volunteers to act out some role-plays to the rest of the group. While you speak, ask the children to 'act out' what you are saying, and then talk with all the children about what they have seen and heard.

- Luna carrying a large toy into school with her bags and struggling to get into the room. Anjana is watching her.
- Kelly, Caio and Evie playing together, bouncing large balls outdoors. Kelly says to Caio that she doesn't like Evie anymore and that Caio is her friend now. Kelly and Caio run away to play, leaving Evie on her own.

Ask the children to tell you examples of when they have been kind and helpful and what it felt like. Tell the children that it feels good to help others and to be kind and thoughtful. Create a 'smiley face' on a piece of paper and allow room in the centre for the children to draw a picture or write some words about when they have been kind. Remember that it is the act of doing this that is important, and not the quality of the picture! Tell the children that you are going to laminate the 'smiley faces', and the children can attach them to the kindness tree (indoors or outdoors).

Teaching tip

Reinforce the fact that other children and adults don't forget acts of kindness – whether big ones or small ones! Thoughtfulness makes our world a much better place.

Messy play

'Three children in nursery have poor speech and language skills. They don't like working with others but they do enjoy playing outside in the mud kitchen. How can we encourage them to speak more and play with the other children?'

Messy play is an important activity as it enables the children to experiment, explore with others and develop physically. It has an impact on cognitive and creative development.

Taking it further

Talk to the children about their favourite recipes and ask them how they could record these for future use by other groups.

Bonus idea ★

Demonstrate to the children how to create potions in plastic bottles using water and food colourings. When made, display them on a shelf in an outside shop. Provide a till and play money.

In the mud kitchen, create activities where the children need to work co-operatively with other children. Provide water, soil, sand, stones, rocks, ferns, leaves, acorns and flowers, and also foods such as lentils, pasta and rice. Give opportunities for the children to collect some of these ingredients in small baskets beforehand. Create a bread oven and provide a variety of sizes and shapes of utensils, bowls, spoons, sieves, pans, baking trays and muffin tins. Provide a sink filled with water and soft brushes for washing up. Dark-coloured chef's hats and aprons can be provided, as well as outdoor picnic tables and chairs.

Encourage and demonstrate to the children how to talk to the others about what they are doing or recall what they did. For example:

- 'We have got some leaves, stones and mud for the soup.'
- 'Toby and Ibrahim made a pizza and put it in the oven. I put the cups and plates on the table.'

Ask the children to use their imaginations. Tell them that there will be people in the outside café. Ask them to work and talk together to make, cook and serve the food. Create visual picture recipe sheets that the children can follow. Attach these at the correct height so that the children can use them if they want to.

Power of nature and understanding

'A child has very low self-esteem, struggles with learning and puts himself down. How can we help?

When children experience difficulties on a daily basis, it is hard for them to feel positive and energised. Children need to be active and to move to learn. Being outside in nature is both comforting and inspiring.

So many practitioners report often seeing 'another side' to a child when they go on a visit outside the setting. The children are not so restricted and are free to explore and investigate, especially if they are in 'green spaces' in parks or woodlands.

One idea is to set the child simple challenges – for example, find and collect a green, blue or brown item, something that has fallen from a tree or something that interests them. Play with the child in question. Encourage more child-led activities. Ask the child to tell you what they would be interested in finding. As they are searching, positively narrate what they are doing. Ask them to tell the other children about their findings.

Encourage the children to freely play outside in nature and enjoy and explore the open space. Ask them to listen to birdsong and give them binoculars to see the birds. Give the children clipboards and paper and ask them to draw any insects they see. Ask them to talk about the similarities and differences between insects. Encourage them to look under stones in the undergrowth and run down hollows, kicking up the leaves. Tell the children to work together and help each other. Encourage them to talk to other groups about things they have discovered.

Teaching tip

The children need to be outside as much as possible, learning in all weathers, wearing suitable clothing. It rejuvenates and improves the confidence and wellbeing of all.

Motivation – improving hand–eye co-ordination

'We are trying to motivate and encourage two children in the setting. Do you have any fun games for improving hand–eye co-ordination?'

The co-ordinated control of hand and eye movement and the processing of visual input to guide and direct the hands are important skills.

Teaching tip

Always encourage children to think of other ideas for games they could play with the 'equipment'. Motivate and reinforce the fact that their thoughts and ideas are valued and appreciated. Encourage two-way discussion. Rather than 'talking at', 'talk with' the children.

Bonus idea ★

Cut out a slot at the top of several small, coloured boxes. Cut out varying pieces of card in matching colours and mix them up. Ask children to race against a sand timer to post the cards into the correct colour boxes. Laminating the cards allows the game to be played again and again, with several children racing the sand timer or each other.

Make 'fishing rods' by attaching a small magnet to a stick with thread. Using coloured card, create an open four-sided box ('pond') for children to dip their rods into. Attach magnets (or paper clips) to small coloured cards at the bottom of the 'pond'. Children try to 'catch' the cards out of the pond. A range of skills can be practised on the cards, such as recognising numbers, identifying 2D shapes, reading simple key words or practising sounds. Pictures can also be attached to the cards. When the picture cards have been 'caught', they can be sorted into groups for discussion and extending vocabulary, for example, pictures at the fair, at the seaside, or in the ocean, or different farm animals, or pets at home.

Another idea is to make 'streamers'. Attach long, brightly coloured ribbons or crepe paper to the end of sticks. Play some music and show children how to spin around, twirling and swirling, looking at and making patterns with the ribbons. Encourage children to make up a simple dance in pairs. Invite them to sit in a circle and ask pairs to demonstrate their dance for around 15 seconds (this keeps the pace going!).

Early speech and language skills

Part 5

Power of singing

'How can we increase the children's vocabulary, particularly of nouns?'

Singing is a powerful tool for both language acquisition and aiding working memory. Songs give young children the time to practise, correctly pronounce and internalise sounds.

Teaching tip

It is important for the children to experience as much as possible. First, check that there aren't any children in the class who are allergic to any of the fruit and vegetables. Then, slice the different fruit and vegetables for the children to see, touch, smell and taste.

Taking it further

Create a laminated 'word mat' from an A4 sheet of paper, showing pictures of the different fruits and vegetables with their names printed underneath.

This is an idea to learn and remember a group of nouns – for this example, different fruits and vegetables. Ask the children to stand in a line and give them a picture card showing a fruit or a vegetable. Ask them to hold it up for the rest of the group to see once the name of the fruit or vegetable has been sung.

For fruits, sing the following song to the tune of Frère Jacques:

> *Apple, banana, raspberry, melon,*
> *Strawberry, blackberry,*
> *Peach, plum, pear, satsuma,*
> *Lemon, mango, cherry,*
> *Orange, lime, grapes, avocado.*

For vegetables, sing the following song to the same tune:

> *Carrots, onions, potato, broccoli,*
> *Cauliflower, cucumber,*
> *Cabbage, sweet potato,*
> *Lettuce, celery, peppers,*
> *Sprouts, leeks, beans, sweetcorn, peas.*

Enjoying books

'I want to help my daughter to enjoy books. When asked to take in her favourite book to nursery, she said that she didn't have one and got very upset. She just doesn't like storytime. What can I do?'

Some children find it hard to sit and concentrate for long periods of time. They want to be moving around. Encourage engagement with books by reading together and playing multi-sensory and interactive games.

If it's easier, let the child hold the book, turn the pages and point to the pictures. In doing so, they become more independent and in control. It might be that the child thought that reading was something that was done to them rather than them playing an active part in it. Tell stories together. You read a page, then the child 'reads' a page. Let them use their imagination so that they are not restricted by the book. For some children, this is the key that opens up their world to books. Try looking at a picture book, encouraging the child to make up a story from the pictures, or retell parts of a book you are reading. See whether the child can make up their own version of the story.

What are the child's interests? Ask them what they want to know more about. Choose books that they are interested in. Even at a very young age, some children prefer factual books to fantasy books.

Could the child pretend to read a book to their soft toys, siblings or even family pets? Find some 'props' that make it even more multi-sensory and enjoyable. Teach the child how to make different sounds and use silly voices. Make it fun.

Taking it further

Encourage the child to make their own book using a scrapbook. They can draw their own pictures and stick some in from magazines, etc. Make it with them. Add 'props' to the story and encourage the child to act it out. This could be made into a story sack that the child could take in to nursery to 'read' to the other children.

Limited vocabulary

'Expressing themselves in full sentences is a difficulty.'

Knowing and understanding words is really important for helping children to talk in sentences and express themselves to adults and other children. To say a new word, the child needs to remember the sounds, the order, the meaning and where it 'fits' in a sentence.

Teaching tip

Just in case everyone wants to play being the 'vet', remind the children that it's important to take turns. Keep repeating and encouraging the children to use the new vocabulary.

One idea is to create structured vocabulary role-plays; in this example, the children take their toy pet to the vet. A range of pets can visit the vet – dog, cat, parrot, snake, rabbit, hamster, tortoise or budgie. Provide a variety of 'equipment' for the children to play with – a pet carrier, blanket, brush, bandages, white apron or overall, weighing scales, small torch, stethoscope, toy thermometer, toy till or card machine, toy computer or tablet, low table, paper towels, etc.

Ask the children whether they have been to the vet and what happened. Sometimes you need to give extra help to the children who don't have a pet. Show and talk with the children about the toy pets and equipment they can use. Reinforce new vocabulary relating to the food their pets eat, where they sleep, details about their habits and exercise and why they are taking their pet to the vets. Is it, for example:

- being sick?
- not sleeping, eating or playing?
- limping (ask them to demonstrate)?

Ask the children to show and tell you what parts of the pet's body might be 'unwell' – paws, foot, leg, stomach, skin, ears, back, neck, shell, nose, teeth, mouth, eyes, tongue, head, tail or feathers. Tell children that they need to tell the vet what is wrong with their pet, and that the vet will probably ask them questions so that they can help and make the pet well again.

Alliteration

'Some children are struggling with their language skills. How can we help the children to listen to and enjoy words?'

Alliteration is the repeating of the first letter of a word (in two or more words). Reading or listening to alliteration in nursery rhymes and stories is fun and entertaining for children. It helps them to develop their phonological awareness and memory skills.

A well-known example of alliteration in a sentence is 'Sally sells seashells on the seashore.' If age-appropriate, ask for volunteers to repeat the sentence and have a giggle with the children! Give them some examples of shorter phrases, such as 'busy bees', 'hip, hip, hooray!', 'wicked witch' or 'creepy crawlies'. Invite the children to say the phrases and talk about which were easier and which were more difficult.

Ask the children to think of a cartoon character whose first name starts with 'd' and is a duck (Donald Duck), a cartoon character whose first name starts with 'm' and is a mouse (Minnie or Mickey Mouse) and a cartoon character whose first name starts with 'p' and is a pig (Peppa Pig). Tell children that you are going to play a game called 'All the pets in a line, can you say which is mine?' Say the name of each animal and ask the children to repeat it (they can do actions as well, such as nibbling for a hamster):

- Hungry hamster
- Slippery snake
- Fidgety fish
- Racing rabbit
- Dashing dog
- Tired tortoise.

Go around the circle asking the children whether they can remember the 'name' for the rabbit, the tortoise, the rat, etc. Reinforce the fact that both words start with the same letter.

Taking it further

Tell children that sometimes you can use two words with the same letter and then change it to a different one. It makes it even more fun. Ask the children to say the words and do the actions:

- Bang, bang, crash
- Hop, hop, skip
- Wiggle, wiggle, jump.

Language games

'I want to play simple games with a group of children to reinforce nouns, use connectives and help express simple needs.'

Sometimes simple games can be altered and played again and again to reinforce language skills.

Nouns game

Tell the children that they are going to play a game about naming animals. A well-known game starts with 'I went to the zoo and I saw a bear'. The next child adds one more animal – 'I went to the zoo and I saw a bear and a parrot' – and so on. Unfortunately, it can become a working memory exercise rather than helping the children to think about different kinds of animals. Make the game different by telling the children that every time they say an animal, you are going to draw it (keep the drawings simple!). Draw arrows between the different animals.

Connectives game

Tell the children that they are going to play a game to use the words 'and' and 'but' in their sentences when they are talking and writing. Tell them that you are going to say the first part of the sentence and they can say the next part. For example, 'I put on my socks and...'.

Expressing needs game

Tell the children that you are going to play the 'Why?' game. You are going to say the first part of the sentence and (as in the connectives game) they can say the next part. Tell them that they don't need to say 'why' – they just think it in their head. For example, 'I want to go to the garden (why?)... to look at the plants.'

Makaton

'Frustration at not being able to communicate is a difficulty for some very young children and for children whose speech is unclear.'

Makaton is an effective language programme that uses signs and symbols to help babies and children to communicate and connect with others and the world around them. The use of Makaton often helps children with hearing difficulties too.

Online training on Makaton is available. However, interactive workshops for practitioners, parents and carers, and other interested partners in the setting carried out by health, education and social care organisations are often the most effective form of training. Speech and language therapists also have training in Makaton.

One practical idea is to teach all the children in the setting – not just those children with SEND – the relevant signs and symbols. It is inclusive and often helps other children who might be frustrated or display inappropriate behaviour with their communication skills. Many children's understanding develops ahead of their speech. By using the Makaton signs and/or symbols displayed on cards, all the children can express their thoughts, choices and emotions.

Some of the Makaton signs and symbols that are likely to be useful include those to mean please, thank you, toilet, sleep, dirty, outside, nappy, hot, finished and home.

Create personalised packs of symbols for children on laminated cards, and make visual reminders in the rooms that babies and children can point to. Create copies for parents and carers to reinforce communication skills at home.

> **Teaching tip**
>
> Signing while speaking to babies and children has been shown to encourage the development of communication and language skills.

Nature and making friends

'A child who has limited speech and language skills is much more communicative and sociable with the other children when he is outside in the garden.'

Children are fascinated by the world around them. The outside world and nature provide great opportunities for play, conversation and making friends.

Teaching tip

Give the children clipboards with pictures of mini-beasts on and ask children to find them – for example, snails, ants and caterpillars. Tell children to draw any others that they find and use their bug collectors so that they can show the other children when they find different mini-beasts and talk about them. Ask the children to tell you why they thought the creature was living there.

Taking it further

Give the children a pair of binoculars, a pen and a clipboard, with a simple bird identification chart attached. Ask the children to put a tick on the chart next to the bird that they spotted. Ask the children to talk about and compare the birds and say how many they saw of each kind. (The same activity can be arranged for identifying different types of trees.)

Children love the freedom of being outside, where they can run, jump, roll and shout. When playing games and activities, they communicate with other children through physical actions, not just by speech and language. This gives them confidence and helps them to socialise with the other children.

Tell the children that they are going to plant some seeds and bulbs and see how they grow over weeks and months. Ask them to tell you what we mean by 'weeks' and 'months'. Talk with the children about what plants need to grow (water, sunlight, nutrients or 'food' from the soil). Ask the children to tell you why they need to put on their outdoor clothing and wellies. Give the children pairs of gardening gloves and gardening tools. Tell them that they are going to work with a partner, in pairs. Ask them whether they can think of examples of other 'pairs' today. If they are stuck, point and give them some hints – wellies, socks and gloves for a start!

Provide seed boxes containing large seeds that can be divided, grouped and stored. Demonstrate to the children how to plant bulbs and seeds. Show them and talk with them about the soil, the compost, bulbs, seeds, seed trays, the coloured plant pots and labels. Give the children seed boxes containing a range of seeds and bulbs and ask children to sort them.

Tell the children that they need to work together to work out which bulbs to plant first, etc. Ask them to count whether they have enough seed trays, plant pots and labels.

Set up a treasure hunt. Hide different-numbered pebbles (from one to 20). Ask the children to find, collect and sort the pebbles into baskets. Create a printed sheet with the numbers on, attach it to a clipboard and ask the children to write tally marks to record the numbers found. Encourage the children to tell you about their findings.

Alternatively, give the children bug collectors, portable jars and magnifiers and ask them to collect any mini-beasts. Can the children give you examples of mini-beasts (snails, worms, caterpillars, etc.)? What do they look like? Ask children to show you how they move. Where do they live (under stones, on leaves, in the soil, etc.)? What do they eat? Encourage the children to look at and compare the different markings on frogs, the number of legs on a woodlouse and a beetle, the numbers of spots on different ladybirds, or the different sizes of worms or spiders.

> **Bonus idea** ★
>
> Give the children a large basket and ask them to collect other natural items – acorns, pine cones, conkers, seeds, stones, flowers, feathers, chestnuts, ferns, sticks, bark and leaves. Ask them to sort the items into smaller baskets and count them.

Meeting with speech and language therapists

'A child has a stammer and is reluctant to talk.'

It is important to work with parents and a speech and language therapist to support a child who stammers.

One of the key objectives of the Foundation Stage is to nurture and develop communication and language skills. Before meeting with all concerned, observe the child and gather information. When do they have a speech problem or communication difficulty? When speaking in front of the group, at the beginning/middle/end of a sentence, or when saying difficult or multi-syllabic words?

Do they know what they want to say but can't express the words? Do they speak differently when they are stressed, tired, excited or unwell? Do they avoid talking when they are upset? What emotions do they show and how do the other children react to them? How does the child then react to the other children?

To encourage the child to have fluent speech, do you need to:

- make changes to the group sizes or membership of the group (include friends to increase comfort)?
- practise jumping or clapping out multi-syllabic words? Sometimes singing them in a sentence helps with fluency.
- talk with the other children about how they can help the child?
- reinforce the child's strengths, achievements and self-esteem?

Teaching tip

At the end of a review meeting, set targets and send out this new information to other staff and practitioners. Agree a date and time there and then to next meet to review the child's individual programme.

Taking it further

Ask the child about what would help them. Sometimes they go away and come back with a simple idea that makes a big difference! Making small adjustments to the child's environment eases communicative stress and can make significant improvements to the child's speech.

Understanding concepts

'A child does not seem to understand concepts; she gives unusual answers to questions and finds it difficult to listen to stories. She will often point at objects rather than speak. What can we do to help?'

Receptive language (understanding what is being said) is key to developing a child's expressive language.

There are a variety of concepts for young children to learn, many concerned with location, descriptions, number, feelings and time. Examples include on/off, big/little, thick/thin, hard/soft, smooth/rough, heavy/light, loud/quiet, tall/short, old/new, more/less, forwards/backwards, old/young and hot/cold.

A well-known way to develop language and understanding of concepts is to read and talk to the children about the illustrations in a book. For example, for the concepts of 'up' and 'down', you could ask, 'Where is Jill?' (Up) 'Jill is going *up* the hill. Where is Jack?' (Down) 'Jack is going *down* the hill.' Another idea is to give the child an instruction (in a sentence) and then 'physically model' what the child needs to do. They can then see the concept in the instruction.

Try placing a range of objects – for example, socks, pictures/drawings, toys, books, containers, etc. (up to ten) – in a box and demonstrate two that show long/short, happy/sad or full/empty.

Ask the child to find other examples of the concepts in the box or in the setting. For example:

- in front of/behind
- over/under
- more/less
- always/never
- same/different.

> **Taking it further**
>
> As the child progresses, reverse the activities – the child asks the practitioner to follow an instruction, such as 'Make a loud noise/make a quiet noise!'

Effective communication

'A child is joining us from another setting. The parents and the speech and language therapist have said that the child can use British Sign Language, but his preferred method of communication is speech. They want him to be as independent as possible. How can we help?'

It is important to gain information from the child's parents, the previous setting and any specialists who have been involved.

Arrange a meeting with all concerned, identifying the needs of the child and how they learn and thrive. Organise training for staff – the parents or a specialist teacher may have provided this before for practitioners. Identify the child's strengths, strategies and methods that work best for them. Sometimes the child will tell you and the other children what helps them to play and learn. Organise regular meetings with all concerned to review targets, making use of the home/setting book for daily communication.

Create ways to find out how the child feels they are progressing, building on your relationship with them. Sometimes, the use of hand gestures, role-play, stickers or cards helps to provide instant feedback. Speak clearly and naturally, facing the child so that they can see your mouth. Speaking too slowly or loudly to a child who is deaf and trying to lip-read will make lip-reading more difficult. If the practitioner is with the children at snack time, make sure that the practitioner does not cover their mouth or eat or drink anything.

Also remember that feelings of loneliness can affect a child's communication skills. Observe the child – are they initiating and taking part in games, conversations and play with other children?

Bonus idea ★

To increase the child's independence, on a table, arrange cards with simple pictures on in task order, such as a pair of scissors (cut out), glue stick (stick on), number in a square (sequence, where to place it) and crayon (now colour in). These simple cards can act as memory prompts for other children too, as it makes them all more independent in their playful learning.

Come to our art fair

'I liked making my monster. My family liked it too!'

For all children, but particularly for children who are experiencing difficulties, it is important for others to see the ability they have in other areas.

Help the children organise an art fair. Do they know what an art fair is? Explain that they will be making models or 'sculptures'. Do they know what these are? What materials (or things) could they use to make them?

Give the children a piece of A4 card. Tell them that their model/sculpture can be made on top of it. (For the actual fair, a base/plinth can be put underneath the card to make it look more authentic!) Ask the children about their ideas and what they are doing (take brief notes for later). Tell the children that each piece is unique. Talk about what that means. Ask children to tell each other about their artwork and give the children help. Sometimes what they started with surprisingly morphs into something else!

Create 'About the artist' cards that can be placed next to children's model/sculpture at the art fair. Include the children's previous comments. Ask the children to give their artwork a name and sign the card. Create posters to advertise the fair, talking with the children about the 'important information' that needs to be included, and make tickets for the fair.

On the day of the fair, display the models/sculptures on top of tables (this makes it look more real). Ask the children to show people around. Beforehand, talk to them about what they liked best about their own and other children's artwork (shape, patterns, colours and materials).

Teaching tip

Take photos. On the tablet, record children speaking about their feelings, emotions and thoughts.

Bonus idea ★

If you also decide on a monster theme, make the monsters more humorous by sticking a pair of large wobbly eyes on them!

Conversation bookmarks

'Reception parents sometimes say that when their children bring a book home, they don't always know the best way to talk about it with them afterwards. How can we help them?'

Many settings encourage parents to read a book with their child and talk about it. Some settings give advice in paper form, on an email or in the parents' handbook on how to listen to the child read or how parents can read to them. However, often there is little advice on talking about specific books and possible follow-on activities — that's where the conversation bookmark comes in.

This is a simple idea that engages the children and makes their reading purposeful and fun. Tell the children that they are going to make some 'conversation bookmarks' or 'talking bookmarks' for the class. Do they know what a bookmark is? Show them a range of bookmarks. Tell them that the class bookmarks are going to be slightly different. They are going to be the same shape as a normal bookmark (what shape is that?). However, they are going to have the title and author's name on them and also 'key words'. Do children know what an author is? Do they know what a title is? Do they know what 'key words' are? Give the children examples. Often, children will know the title and the author of their favourite book, as they have listened to it being read to them so many times!

Show the children three recently read books. Ask the children to put up their hand to vote on which book they would like to choose. Tell the children that they only have one vote!

With the chosen book, keeping it very, very simple, ask the children questions (the questions can vary depending on the book). For example, 'What is the title?', 'Who is the author?', 'What was it about?', 'What happened?', 'Who were the characters (people, animals, etc.)?', 'Where/when was it set?' and so on. Older children can very quickly get familiar with this vocabulary.

Beforehand, create the bookmarks on strips of A4 paper (roughly measuring a third of the width of the paper). Write the above key words/questions in large letters on the bookmarks. Tell the children that the paper is wider than a normal bookmark. Do they know what 'wider' means? Give the children a bookmark and ask them to draw small pictures related to the book on the bookmark, such as a red bus. Collect in and laminate the bookmarks.

Bonus idea

Create a bookshop. The children can select a zippy file (containing a book and bookmark) from the shelves and speak to the 'shop assistant' (a child who has read the book) about it. The children turn the pages over and talk about the pictures, story and what they enjoyed about the book. This game helps to reinforce engagement and a love of books and reading.

Seaside banner

'How can we introduce new vocabulary and encourage the children to be more expressive?'

It is important to make language learning as real-life and meaningful as possible. Use all the senses to learn.

Taking it further

Alternatively, divide the group into two teams – the 'sandcastles' and the 'beach balls'. Give the children a pebble each time they say a correct sentence. The winning team is the team with the most pebbles.

One idea is to make a large banner of the seaside, showing a beach area and the sea. This can be displayed across a wall. The children can then cut out and stick on or make seaside items such as a large crab. In front of the banner, there can be a sand area with real objects displayed. Printed words on laminated cards can be displayed beside the 'objects'. Play a recording of some 'sounds of the sea'. Ask the children whether any of them have been to the seaside and what they did there.

Examples of possible seaside 'objects' for display include: bat, beach ball, beach hut, book, bucket and spade, cliff, crab, chips, deckchair, donkey, fish, fishing net, flip-flops, ice cream, kite, lighthouse, lilo, pebbles, picnic, rockpool, sandcastle, seagull, shells, shorts, starfish, sun, suncream, sunglasses, sunhat, surfboard, swimming costume, T-shirt, towel, waves and windbreak.

Now choose any one of the following verbs: throw, hit, sit, play, swim, eat, catch, build, climb, jump, kick, make, play, push, read or ride. Then say, for example, 'I can throw...' and say a child's name. The child goes and touches/holds up the beach ball (on the display), for example. Ask the child to say the full sentence: 'I can throw the beach ball.'

Award one point for each correct answer. Do keep helping and reminding the children. Keep it simple. If they can, ask them to role-play the action!

Learning languages

'The children are learning simple Spanish words and phrases.'

Multi-sensory methods are particularly effective when learning other languages, and great for ensuring that children with SEND are not excluded.

Use the children's senses – sight, sound, touch, smell and taste. Make cards, play games, sing songs, make up raps, recite simple poems and use role-play. Keep 'overlearning' – repeating and repeating but changing tasks slightly so that the children think that they are doing something new. Make it colourful, interactive and fun!

Greetings and key phrases include 'hola' (hello), 'adios' (goodbye), 'por favor' (please), 'gracias' (thank you) and 'quiero' (I want). One idea is to sing, 'Hola Emma, hola Emma.' Emma sings back to you and comes and shakes your hand. Wave your hand and say, 'Adios Charlie, adios Charlie.' Charlie waves back and says, 'Adios.' If the group have been learning for a while, display some items on a tray, such as fruit and vegetables. Say a child's name, then the name of the vegetable/fruit and ask them to come to the front and ask for that item.

To learn colours, ask children to tell you the Spanish word for blue (azul). Point to it on a printed sheet, cut a blue square out from a second sheet and stick it down next to the word on the first sheet. Alternatively (a little more challenging), ask children to paint the correct colour in the square next to the word 'azul'.

For counting, divide children into pairs and set the timer for two minutes. Tell them that one child is going to roll the dice and say in Spanish how many dots they can see, from one to six, before swapping over.

Teaching tip

The counting game is even more fun if you use large dice. Children need to move around the room and movement helps them to learn better. To make the game more challenging, give the children another dice!

Reinforcement games

'I find that the children need more opportunities to practise and repeat new skills.'

Many children with SEND just need time to reinforce and practise skills before they become secure in their learning. This is known as 'overlearning'. Using cards and games is a great way to do this.

Here are three well-known games with a 'twist'. They can be used to reinforce the children's learning of such areas as colours, shapes, or numbers.

Pairs

Lay out ten cards (five pairs) face down randomly on a table, e.g. pictures of whales, crabs, penguins and dolphins. Take turns to turn over two cards at a time. If the two cards are the same, the player keeps those cards. The winner is the person with the most pairs.

Snap

Play 'Snap!' with two piles of cards, each with the same letters on them, e.g. b, d, m, w, p, q. When a card matches with the first card, shout 'Snap!' This is a great game to play with children who have difficulties with reversing figures and letters, e.g. b for d, p for q, m for w, 6 for 9, etc. Ask the children to finger trace if they are finding it difficult to see the pairs.

Lotto

Create a number of 'boards' (depending on group size) with six squares. Place six different pictures inside each square. Create individual cards to pair with those pictures in the squares. Take turns to take a card from the pack and see whether it matches. The first child to match up all six pictures on their board wins.

Listening skills, concentration and processing information

Part 6

Are you listening?

'The children's listening skills are poor. I sometimes have to repeat what I said two or three times.'

These straightforward ideas will help develop children's listening skills.

Working memory can also be involved. Never give children more than two or three instructions at a time. If the child is struggling, one instruction is enough. Break down tasks into small steps so that the child feels it is manageable.

Create an 'attention trainer'. Reinforce a hand signal, movement, phrase/question or, if appropriate, short piece of music so that the children know this signals that they need to stop, turn and then listen to what you are saying. This multi-sensory approach is more likely to gain their attention.

Provide prompts for tasks, e.g. picture cards for a series of instructions. For new vocabulary, create word mats (personalised words on a sheet of paper that have been laminated).

For individual children whose listening skills you know are poor, say their name and, in your mind, count to three to allow them time to give you eye contact. Say your words slowly and let them think about what you just said, as processing speeds vary for different children. If you have just given instructions for taking action, you will be able to see whether the child is listening. If you need to, repeat it. Keep it short. Don't confuse the child by giving the instructions in a different order.

Sometimes a child is said to have poor listening skills when in fact they have other difficulties. The child could have a slower processing speed. Give them time and observe. Does the child understand what you said? Does the child understand the vocabulary or specific words that you used? Simplify your language. Never assume that they understand. Find out by asking them direct questions, e.g. 'Can you tell me what I just said to you?'

Space city

'I need a practical idea for following verbal instructions.'

Some children have difficulty following a series of instructions. Often, too many instructions are given all at once (with new vocabulary for the child to understand). It is difficult for the child to process the information. Start by giving a single instruction, then build up to one more or occasionally two more (if short).

Tell the children to imagine that they are 'astrokids' and they are going to make their own space city. Tell them to paint a variety of upturned yoghurt pots and unusually shaped junk material. Draw on windows and doors, and attach ramps and launch pads to create space pod homes. Write a different number on the top of each home, for example, from one to 12, depending on the age and size of the group.

With the children, create a large table-top space city runway/roads grid on paper or card. Allow plenty of room for children to put their space pod home on and gaps to move between the homes. For extra challenge, place the numbered pod homes in a random order.

Play in small groups of three to five children. They can play by following instructions to drive their space pod car on the roads or fly their toy rocket. Award a point for each time a child follows the instructions correctly. The winner of the game is the first child to reach five points. For example:

- Fly your rocket above the red pod home and land it (or 'touch down') at number 9.
- Drive your space pod car to the blue home (or, to make it slightly more difficult, to the nearest blue home).

Make instructions more challenging depending on the child.

Teaching tip

Always check the children's understanding of new vocabulary – up, down, backwards, forwards, along, above, below, behind, in front of, sideways, etc. Create your own child-tailored instructions on cards so that you can observe the children rather than trying to think of the next instruction.

Rewards for listening

'How can I motivate the children during a listening activity?'

Sometimes it's really tiring for children when they're listening hard, concentrating and processing information all day.

One idea to motivate children is to give them short breaks by playing a traditional game (with a 'twist'). In this case of 'snakes and ladders', it can be played on a giant board. In some settings, the carpet that the children sit on is in the design of snakes and ladders and can therefore be used as a board. If it is a carpet, the practitioner can demonstrate the rules of snakes and ladders by walking across the board. If they land at the bottom of a ladder, they move up to the top. If they land on the head of a snake, they 'slide' down to the bottom of the snake. The team who wins is the first one to reach the top of the board. The children find this very amusing!

Start by dividing the group into two teams, the red team and the blue team. Going round the square (or the outside of the carpet), ask each child a listening skills question (make it shorter or longer depending on individual need). Be mindful of the children who might have a working memory difficulty, and differentiate the instructions if appropriate. For example:

- Clap your hands three times, touch your head and turn around.
- Hop on one leg four times.
- Walk to the door and shout, 'Sausages!'

If the children have listened and followed the instructions correctly, ask them to roll a large dice. Ask them to tell everyone the number (or how many) and move their colour counter along the squares.

What can I say?

'When we have visitors (children and new parents), some of the children in the setting don't know what to say when they are asked a simple question about what they are doing. How can we help them develop their language skills and confidence?'

All children can be helped to improve their communication skills by talking with them about what they are doing and what interests them. It is important to describe (narrate) to the children what you can see them engaged in and also what you are thinking about, as this models how to talk.

One idea is to tell the children a short story and ask the children what they thought about it. Then model some other 'ways' that they could give their views. For example:

- I liked...
- I enjoyed...
- It was funny when...
- My favourite was...
- It was interesting...

Giving just these few words as prompts enables the children to express their thoughts, views and actions.

Instructional words also help children with structure. Talk with the children about the meaning of the following words and then ask them to think of a sentence using any one of them:

- after
- before
- next
- when
- first
- lastly.

> **Bonus idea** ★
>
> Play the 'Gong game'. Tell the children to sit in a circle. Give a child a gong or bell and ask them to bong or ring it when a child says one of the 'new words'. (Have a giggle with them when they bong or ring it in the wrong place!) Talk about a recent art and craft activity that the children did – for example, making a mask. Go around the circle and ask the children to describe what they did, using as many of the 'new words' as they can. Make it fun!

Newsflash

'Encouraging the children to talk more is a priority.'

It is important to hear the children speaking and listening to others in a range of situations.

Taking it further

Alternatively, give a child a toy microphone and ask them to move around the class talking to the other children, asking them questions (interviewing them) about what they are doing and what they are planning to do. This can be further extended by the practitioner asking the 'interviewer' to tell them what the other children said.

One idea is to create an 'outline' of a TV screen. This can be made by attaching a cardboard cut-out square to two wooden sticks that the child holds in front of them. The child faces the other children and appears to be talking through the TV screen. Depending on the age of the group, tell the children that 'TV reporter [say child's name] is going to tell everyone about what happened today in [the setting].' When first doing this activity, be mindful that some children might be reluctant to join in, but over time their confidence will increase.

Talk with the children about what information might be interesting and give them ideas or 'starters'. For example:

- We went to the park to... (Encourage the child to keep going.)
- Zara and Jayden played in the...
- Today at snack time, the...

Tell the children that they can say as much as they want to and it doesn't have to be just one sentence. If the children's 'newsflashes' are quite short, demonstrate to them how they could be longer. For example:

- Today, blue group made animal masks. I made a lion mask with orange stripes. I liked doing it. It was fun. Toby and Max made elephant masks and we played with them outside.

The children who are listening will learn more new words and link them to build them into sentences.

What's in the sack?

'Do you have an idea for describing or listening to descriptions?'

In this activity, children need to practise using their vocabulary skills and listen to descriptions.

Divide the group into two halves – the 'describers' and the 'listeners'. Ask the children whether they know what 'describing' and 'listening' mean. Tell the listeners and the describers to sit on the floor until it is their turn.

Away from the view of the rest of the group, ask one of the describers to look inside a large black sack containing an item (just put one item in at a time so that the child doesn't get mixed up). Tell the child that it's possible to talk about senses – sight, sound, touch, smell and taste – to describe the item (e.g. a banana, a skipping rope, etc.) to the group. It is important that it is an everyday item that the child is familiar with. Tell the child that they can peek inside the sack to remind themselves about it when they are talking to the children, but they mustn't let the other children see! (This adds a layer of mystery to the game.) Remind the child that they mustn't tell the other children the name of the item; they can only describe it! Start the describer off by telling them that they might want to talk about what the item looks like, what it feels like, where they might find it, what it might do, etc.

Tell the listeners to listen to the description and then ask questions by putting up their hand. The describer will say a child's name, who can then ask a question. Be prepared that some children's descriptions will be quite short to start with, as they are learning new skills.

Teaching tip

Remind the children that if they think they know what the item is, they should ask the describer, 'Is it a...?' Sometimes the children get carried away with listening and asking questions!

Interrupting

'A child in my class can't stop talking about his favourite subject of dinosaurs. Although it is great that he is so interested, he is always interrupting conversations and brings them up at every opportunity. He doesn't realise then that the children are ready to talk about something else.'

It can only be a good thing when a child is knowledgeable about a topic and interested in finding out more information about it. However, if it means that the child is only interested in other members of the group who share the child's interests, it significantly narrows opportunities for interaction with that child.

Teaching tip

Work and focus on encouraging real conversations and making friends in the setting. Create opportunities for imaginative play with the other children. It is likely that the child might find these difficult.

Reward the child's efforts for being so knowledgeable about dinosaurs (or their chosen subject) but start by reducing the time for talking about them. Ultimately, you want to decide on certain times or places for discussion about dinosaurs and to gently steer the child towards concentrating fully on the current activity.

In the meantime, use the child's favourite topic to achieve conversational goals with other children – for example, it's a great opportunity for them to practise asking questions. Invite the group to ask a range of good questions about dinosaurs and then the child who loves dinosaurs can answer them. Ask the children to swap around. Now the child needs to think of good questions that the other children haven't asked about dinosaurs. You can, of course, extend the question idea to cover topics other than dinosaurs.

Other ideas that might help include:

- Set a timer or a buzzer for one minute, which the child can hold in their hands. The child will then feel that they have some control but they can only speak for that amount of time on dinosaurs. Experiment instead with using a large sand timer. Place it at the front of the class. This is often a valuable visual cue. (However, some children are put off by wanting to say more but 'time was running out'.) Smaller sand timers can be used as improvement is made.

- Give the child a record card or star chart, which can be completed at the end of each session. This can acknowledge talking about other topics and also learning to change to another subject when asked. The child can gain positive rewards that are meaningful to them from staff and parents and carers at the end of the day!
- Limit the number of 'props' that can be brought in for 'Show and tell' (this applies to all children in the class).

Taking it further

In PSHE, reinforce with the class that it's good to have one interest but it's important to have other interests as well. You could have an assembly with the children dressing up and talking about some of their other interests.

Time language

'What games can we play to help the children who are finding it difficult to understand time language?'

Children have a deeper understanding of time as they get older and have meaningful experiences.

Taking it further

Tell the children what they are going to be doing during the rest of the day using the new 'time words'. If the holidays are fast approaching, keep reinforcing these time concepts by asking the children whether they know what they are going to be doing in the holidays. Be sensitive to those who do not know.

Bonus idea ★

Create a 'time diary', where photos and other small items can be added to help the children look back at their time in the setting.

Start by talking with children about days, weeks, months and years and what is the smallest amount of time. (Very young children often understand time by mealtimes or the number of 'sleeps'.) Clap out the days of the week and (with older children) the months of the year and discuss what month their birthday is in. Talk with the children about the days they come into the setting and what they do on Saturday and Sunday (the weekend).

Talk with the children about other 'time words', such as this morning, afternoon, lunchtime, today, snack time, after, before, tomorrow, in the holidays, tonight, breaktime, evening and at home time. Ask the children whether they can think of any others.

Draw on an A3 sheet of coloured paper a large circle divided into four parts numbered:

1 Before breakfast
2 At nursery/playgroup/school
3 After nursery/playgroup/school
4 Before bedtime

Create another sheet with pictures on, such as a bed, toothbrush, face, apple, car, shops, telephone, book, etc. Cut out pictures and stick them in parts 1, 2, 3 or 4 of the first sheet. Ask the children to point at their cut-out pictures and tell you what they did before breakfast, etc.

Asking questions

'Poor concentration means that a child in the setting often misses important information.'

As well as teaching the child to keep on task by watching and listening to the practitioners and other children, show the child that they can help themselves by asking different questions.

This is a useful skill for all children, not just for those with poor concentration. Ask the children to give you an example of a question. Ask why it is important for adults and children to ask questions. (The children often give some interesting examples!) Tell the children that sometimes we don't know what to do because we might have been away ill, in another room, playing with a toy or not listening, or people might have forgotten to tell us. Tell them that we can find out by asking 'good' questions. Tell the children that asking good questions is not about asking as many questions as you can but about really thinking about what you need to know.

Ask for two volunteers to role-play a situation where the children are rolling out pastry and the practitioner asks them to tidy up, wash their hands and put their water bottles in their bags. Talk while they act out the role-play situation. Tell one of the children to follow the instructions and ask the other child to carry on rolling out the pastry. Ask the children what would be a good question for the child rolling out the pastry to ask. Talk to the children about their replies and ask for 'starter words' for questions. For example, 'What do I need to...?', 'Do I have...?' or 'Is there...?'

Remind the children to use these starter words. Tell them that you will be watching to see that they ask these types of questions when they don't know what to do!

Taking it further

Print several 'speech bubbles' (as in comics) and ask the children to give examples of question starters. Write the words in the bubbles. These can then be used for a display on asking questions!

Social skills

Part 7

Greetings and routines

'A child who has just joined has poor language and social skills. When he arrives on a morning, he doesn't look at you and just runs into nursery to play on the bikes.'

Children need to learn social skills and understand routines and structure when they are in the Foundation Stage. They need to understand others and express themselves using words, gestures or facial expressions.

Start by showing the children photographs of children going through various routine activities. For example:

- arriving at the setting
- shaking hands at the entrance and looking at the practitioner
- saying good morning
- saying goodbye to their parent/carer or taking off their rucksack
- putting their coat on the peg
- putting their book bag or 'communication' diary in the tray
- going to sit at their 'table/morning activity' or on the floor.

Invite the children to tell you what they can see and what the children are doing in the photos.

Ask for a volunteer and demonstrate to the children how to 'greet' on a morning, emphasising eye contact and how to shake hands. Talk with the children about why they think it is a good idea to do this. Play a game where the children stand in a line by the door and pretend that it is 'morning time' (they love saying hello to their teachers!). Reward and praise the children who are learning this new routine. Talk with parents/carers about the routines.

Stop! Think twice!

'I can monitor the children when they are in one group but when they divide into separate activities it can be quite challenging to help those children who have difficulty with their self-control. Their actions and behaviour can disintegrate.'

When children are listening and focused on an activity and then move on to new activities, they often forget their self-control. Other key times are when they arrive on a morning, when they come in from outside, or at the end of the day when they are tired.

The children need to learn and be shown self-regulation skills. Talk to them about understanding and stopping themselves from thinking and then saying bad or inappropriate things or making impulsive actions. Use role-play to teach them how to take appropriate action there and then.

One of the most important aims of the Foundation Stage is for the children to recognise their feelings and those of other children – and to manage those feelings and actions in order to skilfully interact with those around them. Children need to learn to deal with sometimes difficult situations and maintain emotional balance.

An idea to encourage self-control is to introduce 'Stop! Think twice!'. The children stop what they were going to do and think, 'Is it kind or helpful? Does it make you or them happy? Yes or no?' If the answer is 'no', then holding both of their hands in front of their body or even both of their hands behind their back is something that they can instantly do. It is physically calming and comforting to them. It is a simple idea, but effective.

> **Teaching tip**
>
> 'Stop! Think twice!' creates a 'thinking space' and acts as a signal to other children, and indeed the adults, that the child is focusing on improving their self-control. This is a great observation tool and can be used as evidence that the child is trying to improve.

Non-verbal communication skills

'A child in nursery has difficulty in understanding and using non-verbal skills. It is affecting his communication and social development with the other children.'

Non-verbal skills are an important part of communication.

One idea is to observe the child at different times of the day (dependent on age).
Is the child interacting non-verbally with the practitioners and the other children? For example, are they:

- making appropriate eye contact — looking at someone when that person is talking and then not staring too long?
- moving nearer to listen to instructions, then moving away to carry them out (if appropriate)?
- trying not to bump into or stand too close to others?
- smiling, nodding or using facial expressions to show that they are unsure or excited?
- listening and thinking through what has been said?

Talk with the children and role-play appropriate body language and facial expressions, such as smiling, waving, shuffling to make space for others on the carpet, hand gestures (e.g. putting your upturned hands out in front of you to demonstrate 'Stop!'), kindness to others (e.g. collecting resources for another child) and gestures that show others that they are, for example, hot or happy. Emphasise that all of these examples of non-verbal skills are an important part of communication. Can the children think of other examples?

Playing with other children

'A child has just joined the setting and he hasn't had many opportunities at home to play with other children. He appears to be stressed when he is inside. He is much calmer when he is outside. How can I encourage him to engage with the other children?'

Playful learning indoors and outdoors is central to the EYFS. It helps children to develop their language, executive functioning skills (higher-order reasoning/thinking), collaboration skills and emotional intelligence.

Talk with the children about play and why it is important. Ask them to give examples of different activities and ways of playing. Ask for volunteers and role-play some of these ideas. Encourage opportunities for physical outdoor play. Children need to run freely around outside, throwing balls into hoops, playing tag and chasing each other in a safe environment.

Some children who haven't been used to playing with others just benefit from being shown a few different examples of pretend play. Ask the children to help you role-play these different kinds of games:

- games where the child needs to communicate and work with others, e.g. sailing on a ship with an imaginary crew to an island (making choices, using co-operative play and following orders)
- using creativity and experience to encourage more conversation with and among the other children, e.g. making a den outdoors
- children's choice, e.g. creating a dance or blasting off in a rocket to imaginary planets
- social play, e.g. taking orders and serving customers in a café or teaching others how to make meals in the mud kitchen.

Now encourage them to play and use their imaginations!

Teaching tip

Play is important for children who experience high levels of stress. If the other children in the game are responsive and positive, it can help the child with developing relationships and self-regulation and improving their wellbeing and self-confidence.

Bonus idea ★

Children love to hear their voices. The 'Hear Myself Sound Phone' produced by TTS can help children develop speaking and listening skills and can be used outside.

The café

'How can we reinforce social skills – eating out, table manners and working together?'

Social skills help children to work together, communicating with each other either verbally or non-verbally. They enable them to make choices and use their imaginations to explore, experiment and participate.

Teaching tip

The theme of the café can be changed according to the menu, for example, an Italian café with red and white striped table cloths or a shopping centre café.

Create a café in a corner of the setting, with tables, chairs and a kitchen area. Ask for volunteers to role-play how to:

- lay out the table or cutlery
- choose from the menu
- be polite, say please and thank you
- wait tables and take orders
- check the menu and cook/prepare the dish
- serve the customers.

Tell children that they are going to create a simple menu. Do they know what a menu is? Ask them what they might eat in a café and give examples.

A menu card can be printed with names of the dishes at the top and pictures of the ingredients below. This is helpful to the 'kitchen staff', who 'cook' the meal.

Taking it further

Chef's hats, aprons, serving trays, cooking equipment, a cooker, saucepans and even use of money, a calculator, credit card machine or till make it even more authentic. Food boxes can be made and decorated by the children for the shopping centre café.

Divide the group into 'customers' and 'staff' teams (decide the roles beforehand). Tell them to talk to each other in character, pretending to be all sorts of different customers or staff. Sometimes children who are non-verbal or quieter excel at the role-play and making appropriate gestures, and will often communicate verbally because they are 'in role'. The children have great ideas for making it more real! Swap over groups halfway through and talk with the children about their experiences.

Taking turns

'I love role-plays and talking about things!'

Role-play is a very useful tool to reinforce social skills in the setting. So too are catchy phrases! A well-known example in EYFS of a catchy phrase is 'my turn, your turn'. Very simple but it works!

Gather the following 'props' before you start: threading cards and laces, cookery aprons, rolling pins, 'pretend' dough and pastry cutters. Ask the children what they understand by the words 'taking turns'. Ask the children for examples of when they take turns in the day, such as playing with a toy or using the outside equipment.

Choose two children to act out the role-plays. Explain to the other children what is happening as the two children role-play.

- Role-play 1: A child is threading with laces the only available animal-shaped card and another child wants to do that. What could the first child do? Possible answer: Take turns to thread the card.
- Role-play 2: One child has been rolling out the dough and has used his cutter to cut out some of the dough. A second child is rolling out the dough but there aren't any cutters left. What could the first child do? Possible answer: Give the cutter to the other child so the second child can at least cut some out.

Listen to the children's ideas and discuss and talk with them about other occasions in which they could take turns in the setting.

Taking it further

Create a tally chart for times when the practitioners notice the children 'taking turns'. Do this for short periods as it is quite intense, and if it goes on for too long it can lose its sparkle. Every time a child 'takes turns', praise them and award a tally mark. Encourage the children to take turns being a 'tally mark monitor' too!

Building friendships

'Two children have difficulty with making and keeping friends. They just want to play with their own friends and will react if other children want to join in a game.'

Building friendships and learning to work together is an important part of EYFS. Engaging with the children and helping them to become more aware of social situations and behaviours is vital. Children need to learn how to work with others and develop positive friendship skills.

Start with asking the children questions. What is a friend? Why is it important to make friends? Use role-play that the children can relate to to show how you greet a friend or ask a friend to play. Ask the children, 'What makes a good friend?'

Ask the children to close their eyes and think of a friend. Tell everybody one good thing about their friend. Tell them that it is to be about a child, not an animal or a toy, although they can be good 'friends' too!

Create some cards with a range of pictures of young children on. Laminate and attach them to lollipop sticks. Ask a child to choose and pick up one of the picture cards and hold it up for the rest of the group to see. Tell them about 'Harry' (for example). Include details about what games he likes to play, favourite toys, etc. Introduce a new 'picture card friend', e.g. Aiden. Repeat above but this time ask a child to describe Aiden. Create two more 'picture card friends'. Tell the story and act out how Harry felt:

- when his best friend Aiden went to play with the other two friends
- when Harry lost at a game and someone else won
- when the other friends had better ideas.

Teaching tip

Talk with the children not just about how Harry felt but what he could do: go and play with new people and make lots of new friends, understand that you can't always win, and accept that other people have great ideas too!

Social situations

'A child is always wanting adult attention when we are outside. She has difficulties relating to other children and will often disrupt games.'

Children enjoy playing together, learning about their bodies, the environment and their place in the world around them. Some children need to learn about the use of different behaviours in a variety of social situations, and understand the social rules when interacting with others.

Some children just want to take over other children's games and play their games all the time. They do not understand the effects of their actions. One idea is to use role-play. As the practitioner narrates, ask other children to role-play the following situations:

- How to play with others, take turns and sometimes join in with and play other children's games. Emphasise that this can be fun, different and that there are new ideas to enjoy.
- Understanding winning and losing. Emphasise that when you play games, sometimes you win and sometimes you lose, but the child learns because of it.
- How to control impulses – learning to think first. Reinforce the fact that if you snatch the ball from another child, they might not play with you again. Or if you are unkind and run and chase someone, you might bump into other children and fall over.

Ask the children about how they would feel if these 'situations' happened to them. Ask them to show what 'their face would look like' – children are often good at demonstrating facial expressions! Talk with the children about their ideas and how, very simply, they could solve the problems/situations. Encourage them to act it out. Respond in a caring and understanding way.

Bonus idea ★

Develop sticker cards for 'great playing'. Give the child a card and tell them that they will get a sticker every time an adult sees them playing well with others.

Change of routine

'Some children in my class become very anxious when they hear that we are going to be going on a school visit. How can I help them to get the most out of the visit?'

For some children, a change in the daily routine can be extremely stressful. The more preparation that is done before the visit, the more successful it will be. All children benefit from this – knowing where they are going and the reasons for the visit – but some children need even more preparation.

Teaching tip

Do remind the children that sometimes on a school visit there are a range of different noises, and let them listen to them. Some children can be upset by loud noises, particularly unexpected ones like sirens, buzzers or alarms. If necessary, remind children who are particularly anxious that they will be working with a particular adult or perhaps another child.

Before any change to the routine, talk to the children about where they will be going and whether anybody has been there before with their friends or family. What did they see? What did they do? Where possible, show the children pictures on the screen. Find any pictures from a previous setting visit. Be specific on the following questions:

- How will we prepare/what will we do before we leave?
- How will we travel there? Walking, by minibus, by coach, etc.
- What will we do when we arrive?
- What will we look for or what will we do?
- When do we come back to the setting?

An A4 piece of paper with different pictures on it is useful to take home, as well as a note in the home/school book. Pictures on the paper can include a sunhat, a water bottle, a bag, wellies or a pair of gloves, for example. The children can colour/highlight them, as this all helps to reinforce and remind children what they need to bring and what they are going to do the next day.

Another idea when introducing new places is to make a little picture book. This has the benefit that other family members/friends can look through and reinforce information about the visit the night before. The pictures and information could also be loaded up on to a tablet, enabling the child to 'mentally walk' through their visit, e.g. a visit to the fire station. Include pictures of outside and inside the building, then looking at the different types of equipment and what it is for, what 'clothing' the firefighters are wearing and why, etc.

Remember to use and reinforce sequencing vocabulary – first, next, then, while, etc. – thus creating a 'visual story' in the children's heads.

If this is a regular visit, this picture book resource can be used year on year with other children.

Taking it further

For some children, they are anxious about where they are going to eat their lunch or whether there are toilets. For children, these can be very real causes of worry and concern. Always ask the children whether they have any questions about the visit or whether there is anything else they/we need to know. Sometimes their answers to a question highlight a worry that can then be easily solved.

Transition and moving rooms

'A child in my class becomes very anxious when he needs to move to another specialist area in the school. What can I do to help him? He moves up to Year 1 in September.'

This can be difficult for children who rely on routines and find changes challenging. Sometimes leaving the comfort of the class and going to the toilets can be stressful. Some children will even try to avoid washing their hands and run back to the safety of the classroom.

Teaching tip

Encourage regular visits from the Year 1 staff to the EYFS classroom and invite them to take part in activities not just with the child but with the other children too. In this way, it appears normal and routine, and the child feels that they are not being singled out from their friends.

Preparation and familiarity is key for moving rooms and transition.

- Talk to the children about where you are going to go to, why (it helps to give a reason) and what you are going to do.
- Ask them whether they have been there before (sometimes they have been there because of older brothers and sisters). Ask them about what they saw, e.g. a music room.
- Tell them that you are all going to visit the music room (for example) this morning.

Make use of children's visual skills. It helps some children to see pictures of the room before they go, so point out key features or draw a very simple map with the route on it. For example: 'Here is our classroom. We are going to go through the double doors and along the corridor to the room at the end with the blue door, Class 1G.'

It might be more suitable for the child to visit with a member of staff whom the child knows well (and who knows which features could cause distress). It might also be more appropriate to do this at a quieter time or even after school.

Take photos as you go along or record the complete return journey on a tablet. This has the benefit of being able to be played at a later date, at home or during the setting's holidays (reinforcing and encouraging familiarity).

Take photos of the staff and record their names when you meet them. Before they meet the child, let the staff know information about the child's interests, so that they can ask good questions that the child will be able to answer.

Taking it further

If the child is moving to Year 1, the SENDCo, parents/carers and all EYFS staff and other professionals – e.g. health visitor, speech and language therapist, occupational therapist or educational psychologist – who are working with the child should meet with members from the Year 1 team to discuss the child's needs and implement strategies for September. Use this time as another opportunity for collaboration and multi-agency staff development.

Sharing

'It can be difficult to encourage some children to share. I found that by having a visual reminder, it helped.'

The benefits of sharing need to be constantly reinforced in the Foundation Stage.

Taking it further

Create a visual sharing wall chart where children can go to add on their coloured stickers for sharing. Award a badge at the end of the week for the child with the most stickers. Reinforce the setting's rules about sharing.

One idea is to role-play different occasions when children need to share. Organise the following 'props' before you start:

- tray of coloured construction blocks
- dressing-up clothes
- box with hoops, bats and large balls.

Ask the children to sit down in a circle. Choose two children at a time to act out the different role-plays. Explain to the children what is happening as the pairs act it out.

- Role-play 1: A child has made a tower with the construction blocks and another child tries to snatch it. What could the first child do? Talk with the children about it. Possible answer: Tell the child not to snatch. Say that you were playing with the tower. Tell the second child that they can play with some of the other blocks and give them some.
- Role-play 2: Two children are dressing up and one child wants to dress up in the costume the other child was wearing. What could the child do? Possible answer: Both children could swap over costumes and play a game together.
- Role-play 3: A child was playing a game with the hoops, bats and balls and another child wanted to play with the bats and balls. What could the child do? Possible answer: They could play a new game together.

Identifying patterns and visual skills

Part 8

Patterns, patterns, patterns

'Some children have difficulty identifying basic patterns.'

Identifying patterns helps children before they start learning to write.

Use the whole body and senses to experience patterns. In a hall or large open room, demonstrate (depending on the age of the children):

- How to walk in a straight line. Ask the children to hop, jump or skip out a straight line.
- A 'cross' with both of your index fingers. This can also be drawn on a small whiteboard. Demonstrate walking out a cross and then see whether the children can hop, jump or skip out the shape.
- How to walk in a circle. Ask the children whether they know what a circle is. This can again be drawn on a small whiteboard. Decide on a starting point – for example, in front of the large window – and walk around. Ask the children to hop, skip or jump it.

Ask the children whether they know what 'small' and 'large' mean. Can they show you or (on a small whiteboard) draw them for you? Now ask them to make a small circle by walking around, and then a larger circle.

Walk in 'wavy' or 'zigzag' lines. Talk with the children about what this means. Continue with examples of other common patterns. It is important that the children 'experience the shapes in space'. They need to feel them with their whole body.

Bonus idea ★

On a piece of paper, draw six large squares containing six different patterns, namely various-sized circles, wavy lines, triangles, several straight lines, zigzag patterns and several different-sized squares. Photocopy the paper, cut out the squares and attach the pictures to the sides of two large dice. Roll the first dice. Ask the children to roll the second dice until it matches the first dice. To make it more of a challenge, change the pictures and draw very similar patterns so that the children really have to look and count the shapes to identify whether they are the same.

Visual and spatial organisation

'A group of children have difficulties with the order of letters and words.'

Visual skills and sequential memory skills (following through the order) need to be practised, and children need to remember and recall what they have seen. Spatial organisation and sequencing skills are interconnected.

Never assume that children know that text runs from left to right across a page and from top to bottom. One idea to practise the order and direction of letters and words on a page is to draw on an A4 sheet of paper (from the top of the page) a vertical line of red dots on the left-hand side and a vertical line of green dots on the right-hand side (no more than ten dots from the top of the page to the bottom). Check that the children know which is on their left and which is on their right and what a 'straight line' means. Ask the children to draw a straight line from the left red dot to the right green dot and complete the page.

Some children confuse b/d, p/g and n/u, words such as was/saw or figures such as 6/9 and 21/12. To practise the orientation of letters, figures and words, tell children to use their senses. Give them opportunities to colour in and cut out the shapes of letters, words or figures. Arrange and match wooden or plastic letters on templates the correct way around and ask children to trace them with different fingers. Trace the letters, words or figures in sand or paint them on paper. Give the children coloured chalks or squirty water bottles to write large letters or figures outdoors. Tell the children to walk over the top of them (as this also uses their motor memory).

Teaching tip

To help the children remember which is their left hand and/or their right hand, demonstrate with your hands how a capital 'L' can only be made with your left hand, using your index finger and thumb (so this is your left hand).

101

Spot the difference

'How can we teach the children to really look at objects and "see" the world around them?'

Children's visual skills and their attention to detail can be helped by playing simple spot the difference games.

Taking it further

This game can be played in reverse. On a sheet of A4 paper, the child is shown two simple drawings. The child looks to spot the difference between the two drawings and then 'draws in' the missing line or shape on the drawing that doesn't have it.

One idea is to create a selection of spot the difference cards. It is easiest to create two drawings (black outline drawings or sketches). Make a copy of the first drawing and, on this copy (the second drawing), add an additional black line or shape. Make sure that it is visible for a young child to see. Otherwise, it creates frustration rather than encouragement and success! Stick the two drawings onto coloured cards and laminate them for future use. Create cards that are topic-based, as the children love these!

There are many different topics you could use. For example, for the topic 'different types of transport', any of the following drawings or sketches could be used: bicycle, lorry, bus, car, ship, boat, hot air balloon, space shuttle, and so on.

Talk with the children about the different forms of transport and whether they have been on any of them. This is a great opportunity for the children to use their language skills and their imaginations. So many children have been to the moon!

Eye tracking

'A child is having difficulties forming letter shapes, spacing letters in words and writing on lines, and he also misses lines when following on with a sentence.'

Eye tracking and spatial awareness difficulties can also cause problems with reading as well as handwriting. It is important to speak to the parents and tell them your concerns and observations and ask them to have the child's eyes tested.

Observe the child. Do they:

- turn their head sideways when reading or writing?
- move their head close to the table when drawing, reading or writing?
- turn the paper when drawing lines in different directions?
- have difficulties completing letter shapes?
- write over the top of previously written letters?
- use a finger to keep their place?
- miss out or repeat words?
- mix up/transpose words?

Ask the child whether the letters stay in the same place (or move around), but be wary of asking the child too many questions in case they say 'yes' to everything when in fact it is 'no'. Arrange a meeting with all concerned to discuss these observations. Give the parents examples of the child's handwriting. For children who are struggling, here are two simple ideas to try:

- Commercially available 'reading rulers' (a coloured plastic strip with open line space in the middle) may help the child to read.
- Print and shapes on a white background are difficult for some children to see. Choose pastel-coloured paper such as cream, or pale yellow, blue or pink.

> **Teaching tip**
>
> Sometimes a child will be prescribed colour-tinted glasses by an optometrist to help them see more clearly. Coloured overlay sheets are also available for older children in schools. However, sometimes the children choose their favourite colour rather than the coloured overlays that might help them. Also, be aware that children may not have been checked for colour blindness and parents may not realise that their child can't see different-coloured texts side by side.

I can't find it!

'She couldn't see an item when it was lying on a similar-coloured background or find the crayon in a cluttered stationery drawer.'

Figure–ground perception is the ability to focus on one specific piece of information in a busy background.

Well-known activities to improve figure–ground perception are:

- find the hidden treasure in the maze
- spot the difference between two pictures
- complete dot-to-dot pictures
- simple word searches
- colouring-by-number activities
- follow the path
- a variety of seek and find books – for example, find the mouse hidden on the page (see *That's Not My Fox...* by Fiona Watt).

Children who experience difficulties with figure–ground perception often don't know where to begin, as the visual information is so overwhelming. Start by creating baskets containing items such as toys, gloves, empty food boxes, cutlery or hats. Ask the child to find a well-known item – for example, 'Find a car.' Then progress to finding two items that are the same – for example, 'Find the only pair of gloves.' Encourage the child to look for the differences and then the detail. Identify specific colours and shapes in objects.

Make picture card games. Play a form of Pelmanism – take one card and then turn over up to five other cards, one at a time, until the child finds the matching card. Talk with the child about the differences in the colours and patterns. Demonstrate how the child can develop strategies – for example, when searching for an item on a page, start by looking from left to right and top to bottom.

Words all around you

'How can I make the children more visually aware of information?'

Children need to recognise, read and understand information that is all around them in their everyday lives. By making them more visually aware, it increases their engagement and, ultimately, their readiness for reading, writing and learning.

Explain to the children that pictures, signs and print are important. Print can be words in books that are read but it can also be on signs, in shops, in cafés, in the park, etc. Using your hands, demonstrate with an open book how the print (or words) are usually read top to bottom and left to right but not always! For example, they may start halfway down a page.

Create opportunities for the children to 'read' words around the setting. These are endless: on displays, in children's work or on a tricky words display board, for example.

Give children an A4 sheet divided into eight boxes. Ask them to go on a 'print/word hunt' and write in the boxes examples of words they can find in the setting. (Some will be able to copy the words and others may be able to read or guess them.) Bring the children to the carpet. Talk about their findings. Write these on the class whiteboard or, alternatively, the children can write them on the class whiteboard themselves.

Go on a visit to the local park or shops. On an A4 sheet, print out pictures of street signs, shops, community centres, bus stops, traffic signs, etc. Ask children to tick them off their sheet when they find them. Remind the children that pictures, words and signs can all give information.

Teaching tip

To emphasise why print or words are important, ask what would happen if we didn't have:

- names on clothes pegs or book bags?
- entrance signs?
- fire exit signs?
- a stationery station sign?

Taking it further

Create a print/word awareness activity sheet, where family and children can draw in examples found at home – recipe sheet, greetings cards, etc. – and talk about what the print says.

Forming letters, writing words

'Forming letters and writing words is difficult for a group of children. Different-sized letters are often written all together. What can I do to help them?'

If children can automatically write letters and words, it gives them the freedom to concentrate on what they were writing about.

Teaching tip

Tell the children that letters and words can be printed differently on a page (different fonts), as this can confuse them when they first start writing.

Here are some ideas to support this area of development:

- In a large space, show the children how to move and walk while making different shapes. Start by demonstrating a straight line, then a curved shape and then lines on a slant. This is important, as they have to learn how to slant letters if they are learning cursive writing later on. If appropriate, demonstrate how to move and walk and make specific letter shapes. Tell the children that they need to be careful not to bump into other children. Sometimes they are too busy concentrating on making the letter shapes!
- Use squared paper for the children who are writing different-sized letters all together (poor letter proportioning), as they cannot see the spaces between the words.
- Develop the children's positioning skills (where letters and words are on a page) and their tracking skills (following those letters and words across a page) by giving the children a highlighter pen to highlight words in a text and then on their own writing. This is an effective visual tool.

Tell the children that they need to slow down and keep practising. Refining their movements will extend their motor memory and concentration skills.

Early literacy and mathematical skills

Part 9

Rhymes, rhymes, rhymes

'For the children with phonological awareness difficulties, it can be difficult recognising and generating words that rhyme, e.g. sat, hat and cat. We play games to identify the odd one out, e.g. bat, fat, sit and pat, but what other games could we play that are more interactive and fun?'

Singing and listening to nursery rhymes and songs repeatedly helps to emphasise rhythm and rhyme in language.

This is an idea to encourage children to get involved. Where there isn't a physical action associated with the song, ask the children to think of one. Ask the children to stand up to start.

Say, 'I'm thinking of a word that sounds like 'tall'. Then say the line 'Humpty Dumpty sat on a...' (children say 'wall'). Say, 'I'm thinking of a word that sounds like 'ball'. Then say the line 'Humpty Dumpty had a great...' (children pretend to fall down and say 'fall'). Say, 'I'm thinking of a word that sounds like 'hen'. Then say the line 'All the king's horses and all the king's...' (children say 'men'). Say, 'I'm thinking of a word that sounds like 'ten'. Then say the line 'Couldn't put Humpty together...' (children say 'again').

Following this example, the children will also be able to recite the rhymes and do the actions to 'Twinkle, Twinkle Little Star', with the emphasis on 'star', 'are', 'high' and 'sky', and 'Incy Wincy Spider', with the emphasis on 'spout', 'out', 'rain' and 'again'.

> **Bonus idea** ★
>
> The children sit in a circle. Pass around a 'surprise box'. Each child takes out one item. Inside the box there are two items that rhyme with each other. (Make sure no more than two items in the box inadvertently rhyme with each other!) When the box has been passed all the way around the circle, the children stand up to find their 'rhyming pair partner'. When they have found them, they sit down. In pairs, they show and tell what their two rhyming items are, e.g. sock/lock (a sock and a small padlock), hat/cat (a hat and a toy cat), etc.

Initial sounds

'This idea helps children who can't hear the beginning sound in a word.'

Identifying the sound at the beginning of a word (the initial sound) is a common phonological awareness skill that needs to be mastered.

The well-known game 'I spy' is often played to practise this skill. 'I spy with my little eye something beginning with W.' The children then look around the setting and say, for example, 'Window!' There are also games with different plastic letters, where various objects are placed on a board and the children have to find the object that has the same initial sound as the plastic letter at the beginning of its name.

Talk about the sound at the beginning of words, e.g. listen to the word 'Sunday'. It starts with the /s/ sound. Ask the children to say some more words that start with the /s/ sound. Pass around some hand-held child-friendly mirrors and ask the children to say the sound. Ask them to watch and feel how their lips and tongue move.

In a treasure chest brimming with other objects, place a few /s/ objects inside, e.g. soap, snake (a toy snake!), etc., and ask the children to find them. Talk about them. Can they think of any other /s/ examples?

Taking it further

Give the children a clipboard with an A4 sheet attached to it that has been divided into eight boxes. Explain to the children that there are other /s/ objects hidden around the room. Ask children to search and find them. Ask the children to draw a picture of the object in one of the boxes on their worksheet. Write 'S' next to it. Always check before the children come into the room that you have plenty of 'almost visible' /s/ objects!

Let's read a story

'I am a newly qualified teacher now working in Reception. I find it difficult when I am reading a story to have all the class's attention. Some sit and shuffle. How can I make it more interesting?'

Learning in EYFS is primarily based on experiences. Multi-sensory methods and ways of teaching benefit all the children in the class, using, for example, their visual, auditory and kinaesthetic skills.

Always read the book first; never just pick one up. Children can tell whether the practitioner knows the story and has read the book before. The book could be linked to a class topic. Identify the language that you want to focus on, as well as the theme, the characters, the storyline and the sequence of events. It might be that you are reading the book as a talking point because of something that happened in the day. It might be about reinforcing class values – being kind, taking turns, helping others or celebrating similarities and differences.

Is it a long story? If so, read it over two sessions rather than hurrying through it and risking the children losing focus. This gives an opportunity at a later date for further discussion, and you can also assess what the children have remembered and understood.

Show the children the cover, and point out the title and author. Ask the children whether they have heard any other stories by this author. Ask the children what they think the book might be about. Have they read any other books on this theme/topic, e.g. on explorers or dogs?

As you are reading, stop and comment on the text or pictures and ask questions. Remember to give the children plenty of time to look at the pictures and talk about them. It takes time for the children to really look and think about what they are hearing and understanding, and sadly this activity is sometimes rushed. Give them time to ponder. The questions they ask and answers they give will be more thoughtful and insightful. Ask questions that use their prediction and thinking skills:

- What do you think might happen next?
- What if...?
- I wonder how many...?

Relate what you are reading to the children's experiences and their emotions.

- Do you remember two days ago, when we...?
- How do you think they felt when...?
- What did you enjoy most about...?

Taking it further

Tell the children that you are going to create your own class reading book. Tell them that it's a second book (or sequel), based loosely on the characters in the book that you have just read. Reinforce that the children don't need to create new characters, as the characters are already there. This saves time and gives a helping hand to the children who don't know where to begin with stories. They can start getting into the action straight away!

Improving comprehension

'A few children in my class listen to stories but don't always seem to understand or become involved in them.'

Improving comprehension and language through talking about stories helps children to understand the world around them. Strategies can be used to encourage children to think more critically. It has been shown that guided reading improves their thinking and learning power.

One idea is to read a story and then look critically at its structure. Ask the children questions that will divide the story into four parts. Here is a brief outline of an example story:

- Barney the dog was running in the woods and got lost. Charlie, his owner, was calling him – 'Barney, Barney!' – but Barney didn't come back. Barney had fallen down a hole and his leg was trapped in a tree root. Barney made friends with a rabbit called Moss, who used his hind (back) legs to make the hole bigger, so that Barney could be free. Barney thanked Moss and went back to see his new friend every day.

Ask the children questions:

1. What was the story about?
2. What was the problem? (Further question: Why did it happen?)
3. How was the problem 'fixed'? (Further question: What other ideas could you think of to help Barney?)
4. How did it end? (Further question: Do you think it was a good ending? Could you think of a different ending?)

Always explain new vocabulary to the children. If they don't hear it, they'll never use it! Understanding and using language is key to being able to communicate with others.

Bonus idea ★

Create more simple stories with the children's help on a variety of topics – at the seaside, going to the pond, pirate island, etc. Include new vocabulary and simple comprehension questions. The children's spoken words can be recorded, or written down and then made into small booklets that the children can decorate. The children love to see their ideas being used and appreciated. The small booklets are a resource that can be lent out or used with future groups.

Using a 'circular' piece of card, draw and divide it (using a ruler and pen) into quarters, numbered clearly with 1, 2, 3 and 4. Give the children one card each and ask them to draw pictures in the four quarters. Demonstrate what 'quarters' means.

- Q1: Barney the dog and trees
- Q2: Barney trapped in a hole
- Q3: Moss the rabbit helps
- Q4: Barney and Moss.

It doesn't matter about the quality of the drawings; it is about what they represent to the child. The card circle can then be folded down into one quarter and then opened out. A wooden lollipop stick can be firmly attached to the centre and then made into a 'story umbrella'.

Taking it further

Ask the children to twizzle the 'story umbrella' around and tell you what happened in picture 1, picture 2 and so on. Check their vocabulary and understanding. Reinforce the structure of the story. Tell the children to ask questions and think like this every time they hear stories, as it will help them to understand.

Beat it!

'How do I help the children hear syllables in spoken words?'

Hearing individual syllables (or beats) in words is an important part of phonological awareness and developing the child as a reader.

One idea for hearing and identifying syllables in spoken words is to ask the children to sit in a circle and then clap and model a name. For example, Ra-chel = Rachel. How many syllables are there? Two. Go around the circle and encourage the children one by one to clap their name and then say how many syllables it has. Ask the children whether they can think of any other examples.

Another idea is to play the 'humans game'. Unwrap a large roll of wallpaper and ask a child to lie down on it, then draw around them. Do this five times on separate sheets. Ask different children to write the number 1 on the first outline sheet, 2 on the second outline sheet and so on, until all five sheets have a large number on. Ask a child to say the name of one person in their family. How many syllables are there in the name? Ask the children to tell you which one of the five outline sheets the practitioner needs to write the name on. Tell the children that they can choose different colours for the different names. Ask them whether there are names that have more than five syllables in them. Ask them whether the practitioner will need to make more outline sheets.

Bonus idea ★

Play the drumming game. You can use drums but pots and pans do just as well. Say the name of an animal and ask a child to repeat the name, banging their drum the correct number of times. Are they right? Every time the child gets it right, award them one point. At the end of the game, add up the scores but keep your own tally too! It's also a good idea to write out your long list of animals before you start.

Meaningful learning

'For children who find literacy and maths quite difficult, how can I make it more fun?'

Children will find it more interesting when they can see that literacy and maths are a meaningful part of their lives. Make indoor and outdoor experiences fun, relevant and something they can instantly become involved in.

To start with, put yourself in the position of a child. Write a list of the activities they do from the moment they arrive at the setting:

- place wellies on the outside rack
- put water bottle in tray
- take out home reading book from bag and place that and the bag in separate boxes
- hang up coat, gloves, scarf, etc.
- playing morning activities, etc.

Think about using these activities as opportunities for making the children's learning more meaningful to them. What opportunities are there, for example, for counting, sorting, comparing and understanding the value of numbers? One idea would be to create simple sorting activities with their own coloured, patterned or different-shaped gloves, scarves or socks (but do first make sure that they are all named!). Easy-grip tweezers can be used to scoop, sort, tweeze and transport soft pom-poms into tubs, or pebbles can be sorted and sequenced according to shape, colour and texture.

Taking it further

When children are getting ready for snack time, encourage them to use their problem-solving skills when arranging the room. Ask questions: Six more children are joining us today from Green Room – how many children will there now be? How many chairs and tables do we need? (Some children can answer this straight away!) Do we have too many? Do we need to take some away? Are there enough? Are the chairs in the right place/position? How could we make it better?

Garden centre

'A group of children are having difficulties with sorting, counting and comparing. What practical activities could we do to help them?'

Create a 'garden centre' area. This provides huge opportunities to further the children's mathematical understanding through learning by doing.

Taking it further

Ask the children to record on a tally sheet the group's favourite fruit from a choice of fruits. Count, compare totals and make a pictogram of the results.

Set up a 'garden centre' with a range of items (real or toy) on tables such as flowers/plants, fruits and vegetables, packets of seeds, bulbs in pots, trays, trowels, a hose, a wheelbarrow, aprons and a till or card machine. Here are a selection of 'garden centre' ideas:

- Sorting and categorising: Check that the children know the difference between a vegetable and a fruit. Ask the children to put all the fruits together in one basket and all the vegetables in another basket. Ask the children how they could be sorted in different ways.
- Counting: Count the vegetables and the fruits. Count the pots. Ask the children to give them to you one at a time, then ask them to give them to you two at a time. Alternatively, count and then separate a group of three or four plant pots in different ways (for a group of four: 1+3, 2+2, 3+1). Ask the children whether the total is still the same.
- One-to-one correspondence: Put one bulb from the bag into each of the pots.
- Sequencing: Number the pots. Ask the children to put a bulb in the number 5 pot, etc., or ask the children to arrange the pots in numerical order.
- Comparing: Compare two groups of flowers, adding one more flower and saying when they have the same number.

Mealtime maths

'Children like to help with the snacks and drinks and when we go on visits. How can we use this time to help them with maths?'

Preparing the morning snack or sorting food when going on a trip are both ideal opportunities for maths.

Here are a range of ideas:

- To start, make sure that everyone has washed their hands thoroughly! Ask the children to place the various 'fruits' and 'snacks' onto the trays. Which fruits are the same? Which ones are different (e.g. red apples and green apples are the same, peppers are different)? Why?
- Ask them how many plates they need. If they don't know, ask them to count the children sitting at the tables. If they count out too many, ask them how many less they need. They might need some help with that calculation (if it's a large group) but some children might be able to do it!
- When you are halving and quartering the fruit and vegetables, e.g. apples, pears, peppers, etc., ask the children to tell you how many pieces there are now.
- Arrange six apples on a tray and ask children how many there are. Ask them to see the numbers that are 'inside' six. (Hopefully they will see 1+5, 2+4, 3+3.) Will the addition calculation still add up to six if you swap the numbers around? Ask them how they know that. Can they show you why? Rearrange the six apples into a different pattern and ask how many there are now. How do they know?
- Ask the children to arrange the apples into twos and count them. Can they carry on counting in twos? If it's an appropriate time, do the same for threes. Talk about doubles: 3+3.
- Ask the children whether the piece of bread or cracker is 'smaller than' or 'larger than'...?

Construction site maths!

'I like playing outdoors. I like playing this game on the building site. I like counting and building the walls.'

This is great for reinforcing the understanding of numbers in a natural, fun and purposeful way. Children can also use their everyday language to talk about mathematical topics.

Taking it further

Provide toy bricks to construct a wall, tower or other building. Alternatively, create a 'driveway' on the ground by drawing out the pattern of the blocks on a large sheet of card (perhaps a herringbone pattern). Make the individual 'blocks' from card and laminate them. Number the individual blocks so that the child can count and match them to the numbered blocks on the large sheet of card or the 'driveway'.

Encourage the children to sing counting songs and rhymes. These help to develop the children's understanding of number. Create your own versions of counting songs and rhymes. For example, using the well-known rhyme 'Buckle my Shoe':

> One, two, build something new
> Three, four, add a door
> Five, six, pick up bricks
> Seven, eight, lay them straight
> Nine, ten, we're building again!

When the children start playing at the construction site, tell them that they need to always check and count that the correct builders' 'tools' are stored in the right places. This gives the children another reason to count. A good idea is to have the storage nearby or attached to a fence, with the corresponding numeral next to it, e.g. 4 toy spades, 5 toy brushes, 3 tool belts, 1 toy cement mixer, 6 hats, 6 overalls, 2 wheelbarrows and 1 crane.

Create a sandpit area with the cement mixer inside, as well as other containers and toys, e.g. diggers, trucks and dumpers. The children can use everyday language to talk about and compare size, position, weight and distance. On a laminated A4 sheet of paper, show visual instructions for how to make the ideal cement using different-sized containers. Encourage the children to make comparisons between quantities and numbers, e.g. 'more' and 'a lot'.

Encouraging independence and personal organisation skills

Part 10

Becoming independent

'There is a difficulty with a child who has relied on others to get her dressed and feed her, rather than doing it herself.'

If some children who are able to learn self-care skills don't want to, this limits their experiences, not just in but outside the setting as well – for example, difficulties with visits, going to birthday parties and sleepovers at family or friends' houses.

Start by talking with the parents about what the child can do at present. Discuss with the parents some of the areas that you might be going to focus on in the setting to encourage the child's efforts at independence. For example:

- arriving at nursery (hanging up coat, bag, etc.)
- getting ready for activities (finding equipment, working together)
- self-care (toileting, washing hands)
- getting changed
- making choices (drinking/eating at snack time and lunch)
- packing a bag to go home.

Establish routines and give the child time to complete tasks. Identify a 'helper buddy' who will give the child prompts or who the child might copy (at first). Give choices between healthy food options and provide objects or pictures to support those choices – for example, a daily menu. Involve the child in preparing food and pouring drinks. Ask the parents what 'strategies' and rewards worked at home to encourage more independence. Identify equipment that could be used to motivate and sustain concentration – for example, when getting dressed, the use of a time tracker or large sand timer. Create rewards for achievement – especially what might be seen as rewards for small things, which often build into the major achievements.

I'm stuck!

'Some children don't know what to do when they're stuck or don't understand something.'

To make mistakes and learn from them is normal; so too is teaching young children that everyone 'gets stuck' at times and doesn't understand, but there are things that a child can do to help themselves and to enjoy their achievements.

It is often assumed that children instinctively know what to do, but they actually need to be gently shown, modelled examples and encouraged to be more independent and start to think for themselves with kind adult support. Reinforce to the children that the adults are there to help them. Tell the children to ask for help and talk with them about *how* they can ask for help – for example, going to find an adult, putting up their hand, etc. – and who could help them. Encourage the children to give examples of when they have needed help and what happened. Were they stuck? Did they not understand what they needed to do next?

Talk about how sometimes asking another child what they need to do or watching other children helps them to understand. Reinforce that sometimes it helps to just ask the adult to tell them again what they need to do. Talk about how to ask questions and emphasise the 'helper starter questions':

- Who?
- What?
- Where?
- Which?
- When?
- How?

Encourage the children to give you examples of questions they could ask.

Teaching tip

Working on improving the children's vocabulary and self-esteem is important. Independence skills and the confidence learnt in the Foundation Stage carry right through to their school life and beyond.

Following instructions

'How can we encourage the children in Reception to follow simple instructions and then work things out for themselves?'

Children can become more independent in their learning by experimenting and finding answers to questions.

Teaching tip

To make it easier to plan their movements (if the children are experiencing sequencing, directional or spatial difficulties), write on the cards ' L' for left and 'R' for right, or colour-code the cards.

Taking it further

Create animal/bird footprints or really giant-sized human ones! Lay them out on the floor and use them for other activities. Ask the children, 'While we have been away, who has been visiting us?'

Play the 'footprint game'. Standing on a piece of coloured card, trace around a child's feet (or an adult's feet to make them larger). Trace around the left and the right foot. Cut them out so that you can see the outline. Draw on circles for toe pads and heel pads so that they look like the imprint of feet. Make multiple copies of both feet (depending on the number of children in the group and the length of the activity).

Select a child and ask them to walk, placing their left foot forward, then their right foot forward. Ask the children to show you which is their right foot and which is their left foot. Demonstrate how to play the footprint game by placing the card feet on the floor – right, then left, then right, then left, etc. Show the children how the footprints are not side by side but a little distance apart and slightly above each other. Demonstrate a 'step/stride'.

Following these instructions, ask the children to work in pairs, creating a simple walk. Can the children test the 'pattern' to see whether it works by standing on the footprints? Are the left and right footprints in the correct place? If they are not, ask the children to work together to solve the problem. Ask the children to try out different ways of making the walk more difficult.

Help with organisation

'Bags, coats, jumpers and socks all get lost, and at home time it's a race to find her belongings.'

Many children have poor planning and sequencing skills; they get easily distracted from tasks and they struggle to get ready on time. For some young children, this will improve as they learn, grow and develop, but for others they need to be shown how to be more organised. Using simple memory joggers and establishing routines do help and support children.

Start by talking with parents and carers about routines that are practised at home – waking up, getting dressed, eating, going to the setting, etc. – and working together on the 'new routines' that will support the child in school. If appropriate, talk with the child about what they find difficult. Many children say that they don't know what they need to do and how to start – for example, getting ready for games, packing their bag, or what to do for tidy-up time.

Physically model and 'walk out' routines – for example, what to do first, or where to go to collect/tidy away clothing or equipment. If it helps, use sequential language – 'first', 'second' – or, if more appropriate given the age of the child, use 'start by', 'then', 'next', etc. Ask the child questions to check their understanding or ask them to show you.

Sometimes having a 'buddy' helps – another child who will help the child until they can be independent. Many children learn by copying routines over and over again until they become automatic.

> **Bonus idea** ★
>
> Use as many multi-sensory memory joggers as possible: visual pictures of tasks in sequential order attached to the child's activity tray, peg or basket; identified zones in the setting where the child knows to collect equipment from; or colour-coded storage containers for collecting materials needed for a task. 'Talking tins' and 'electronic cards', where a simple message can be recorded, are excellent independent memory joggers, or try buying items such as 'Talking pegs' or 'Sound lights' from websites like TTS.

Improving interaction

'We have been asked to increase the quality of the interaction between practitioners and the children. How can we do this?'

Encouraging the children to be more independent and improving their communication skills is key to their development in EYFS. Create many opportunities for the children to communicate their thoughts and ideas and give them time to make choices and express their needs.

Teaching tip

Follow the child's lead and take up their ideas. Tell the other children about one child's idea and encourage them to think of other good ideas that could also be used.

Taking it further

As the group move to go to their activity, ask them why they chose that activity. Responses can range from 'I liked it' to 'I want to make a large green house with windows with Jehan.'

Increase playing time with the children. Encourage more child-initiated activities. Listen to their thoughts and ideas. Show the children how to listen through giving good eye contact, using natural gestures, movement, facial expressions and being interested. Use the time for observation as well. Give the children time for thinking and wait for a response. Repeat what the child has said or ask questions – more open questions than closed questions:

- I wonder what would happen if we poured some water in? (open question)
- What should we do next...? (open question)
- Would you like to play with the next puzzle? (closed question)

Always respond to what the children say and extend their language: 'Yes, the red ball – there are two more red balls in the corner of the room.'

Make small cards with either the children's names on or their photo and ask them to find their own card. Create 'choice posting boxes' – for example, for choosing one of three activities from construction toys, planting bulbs and sand tray. Ask the children to post their name card into the posting box (with the appropriate activity picture displayed on the box). Once all the children have chosen, select a child to say the names of the children for each activity.

Choices

'Sometimes the teacher says, "Choose the table you would like to work at." I like making things and drawing.'

It is important to encourage the children to be more independent and learn to make their own decisions. By giving them choices, it motivates them to do this.

Create a simple survey of the setting. When and how do you offer choices to the children in their indoor and outdoor learning? What other choices and activities could be offered? Ask your team and the children for suggestions. The children often have simple and novel ideas.

Are the children always directed to one table and then moved to other tables to complete all the day's activities? Can they choose? Can they choose whether they play and work indoors or outdoors for different activities? The children love to see that their ideas are welcomed, listened to and acted upon. One idea that is really successful is to create a treasure chest that is known as the 'children's ideas treasure chest'. This is where they can choose from a range of learning games (created from their suggestions). All games need to be included in a zippy pocket file for accessibility and organisation. Some ideas include:

- Threading and lacing laminated templates of favourite vehicles or animals.
- Building blocks and a simple diagram to follow to make a castle (or build your own and draw the diagram/picture!).
- Make up a story about two finger puppets and then perform it to a friend. Swap over.

Stick an 'Idea by...' card on the zippy pocket file and ask the child to sign it.

Teaching tip

Reinforce that when it is the end of the game and tidy-up time, it is their responsibility to put all the 'parts' back into the file and put it in the chest for the next child to enjoy.